DUAL ZONE
AIR FRYER COOKBOOK:

Healthy & Tasty Dual Zone Air Fryer Recipes for your 2-basket Air Fryer

By
Chris Chapman

Leave a review about our book:

As an independent author with a small marketing budget, reviews are my livelihood on this platform. If you enjoyed this book, I'd really appreciate it, if you left your honest feedback. You can do so by clicking review button.

I love hearing my readers and I personally read every single review!

TABLE OF CONTENTS

INTRODUCTION

The Dual-Zone Air Fryer is a super cool kitchen appliance that changes how you cook your favorite food. It allows you to make more than one dish in a single cooking cycle because it has two separate cooking zones. So, if you want crispy fries and tasty chicken wings, you can have both, and they will turn out perfectly. This air fryer is great because it makes your food just right with precise temperature control and rapid air circulation techniques. Say goodbye to greasy and unhealthy fried food, and say hello to a healthier and more convenient way of cooking with the Dual-Zone air fryer.

This cookbook is what helps you become a master in using the dual-zone air fryer. In this cookbook, you will find plenty of great meal recipes that you can cook for your family and friends. Using this cookbook, you will also learn how the air fryer works and how to make delicious dishes. In this cookbook, you will go on a journey to discover different types of dual-zone air fryer recipes worldwide. You will also find delicious and healthier fried food recipes and new, yummy ideas that will surprise your taste buds.

This cookbook is loaded with hundreds of mouthwatering Air fryer recipes. The recipes in this cookbook come from different categories, like delicious breakfast, lunch, appetizer and side dish, fish and seafood, poultry, meat, vegetables, and desserts. All our recipes are created to excite your taste senses while giving you abundant essential nutrients.

Why use the 2-Basket Air Fryer Cookbook?

The dual-zone air fryer is one of the most innovative smart cooking appliances and comes with two separate cooking baskets, significantly enhancing your culinary journey and cooking experience. Explore how this innovative appliance saves users time and effort by cooking multiple dishes simultaneously without worrying about mixing flavors or compromising temperature settings.

The dual-zone air fryer uses smart technology to cook your favorite food just right. It does not matter if you are frying, baking, roasting, or grilling your food. It allows you to make your food exactly how you like it without any trouble. The settings for each basket can be changed to ensure each dish cooks perfectly.

Benefits of the dual-zone air fryer

The dual-zone air fryer is one of the most modern and revolutionary cooking appliances. It is one of the ideal air fryers for the whole family. The air fryer has several features and benefits, some of which are as follows.

Multifunctional Cooking appliances: The dual-zone air fryer is a versatile kitchen appliance that allows you to cook two different dishes simultaneously. It is not only just an air fryer but also offers multiple cooking functions, such as max crisp, roast, reheat, bake, and dehydrate. While using this appliance, you never need to buy separate cooking appliances for each cooking function. The best part of the dual-zone air fryer is that you can simultaneously cook two different dishes using different functions.

Healthier Air Frying: If you enjoy fried food but want to cut down on calories, the dual-zone air fryer is one of the great choices. It cooks your food using 80% less fat and oil than traditional deep frying. Less fat means fewer calories, helping you stay healthy and fit. With this air fryer, you can make tasty and healthy dishes at home without sacrificing the deliciousness of deep-fried food.

Quick and Even Cooking: The dual-zone air fryer uses hot air circulation technology with the help of a convection fan to cook your food evenly and faster. It reaches temperatures up to 450°F. It is 70% faster as compared with the oven. This makes it the perfect choice for cooking the main dish and a side dish for larger families. For example, it can make crispy French fries in 12 minutes, thanks to rapid hot air circulation.

Big Cooking Space: The dual-zone air fryer can cook a lot of food at once. It can hold up to 7.6 liters of food in both food baskets. Plus, you can cook two different things at the same time. For example, you can make about 4 pounds of French fries and chicken wings together.

Preserve Nutrients: The dual-zone air fryer cooks your food by swirling hot air around the food basket. This method keeps the nutritional value of your food intact. When using the traditional deep frying technique, most of the nutrients in the food get lost.

Easy to clean: The interior of the dual-zone air fryer comes with a non-stick ceramic coating. It makes your day-to-day cleaning tasks faster and easier way. The metallic cooking baskets are dishwasher safe; you can easily wash them in the dishwasher.

How does the dual-zone air fryer work?

The dual-zone air fryer works on a dual-zone technology. In this cooking technique, both the cooking areas are working independently. They are equipped with a heater and cyclonic fans. It allows you to cook two different dishes simultaneously on a different program, time, and temperature settings.

How to Use a Dual-Zone Air Fryer:

1. Plug in the air fryer and turn it on.
2. Put your ingredients in one of the food baskets (Zone-1). If needed, add a crisper plate at the basket's bottom. Then, fix the basket into the air fryer.
3. Repeat step 1 for the other cooking zone (Zone 2).
4. Pick the right program for each zone based on your recipe.
5. Change the time and temperature settings using the TIME and TEMP buttons.
6. Press the Start/Pause button for each zone separately to start cooking.
7. When one zone is done, the display shows «End,» and the other zone keeps cooking.

Functions

The dual-zone air fryer has some pre-set cooking functions, as follows.

1. **Air Fry:** Air frying is a healthy way to cook your favorite food using very little fats and oil. It makes your food crispy on the outside and juicy on the inside. Using this function, you can air fry things like French fries, onion rings, and chicken wings without changing the taste and texture like deep fried food.
2. **Air Broil:** Air broiling cooks your food closer to the heat, making it crispy and melting toppings over it. Using this function, you can broil burgers, melt cheese on nachos, brown casseroles, and get a perfect finish for sandwiches, fish, steak, and meat.
3. **Roast:** The roast function is great for cooking big pieces of meat, poultry, and veggies. It turns your dual-zone air fryer into a roaster oven, making your food tender and tasty dishes. Roasting is a dry cooking method that gives your food a brown texture and enhances its flavor.
4. **Reheat:** Use this function to reheat your leftovers without overcooking. It is better than the microwave oven because it warms and crisps your food, making it tastier than before.
5. **Bake:** This function turns your dual-zone air fryer into a convection oven. In this function, hot air circulates the food basket to bake cakes, cookies, and desserts to bake your food perfectly.
6. **Dehydrate:** Use this function to dehydrate fruits, veggies, and meat slices. It removes moisture from food and preserves it for longer.

Kitchen Conversion Chart

Ounces (oz) to Grams (g)

1 oz	=	28.4 g
2 oz	=	56.8 g
3 oz	=	85.2 g
4 oz	=	113.6 g
5 oz	=	142 g

Pounds (lb) to Grams (g)

¼ lb	=	112.5 g
½ lb	=	225 g
¾ lb	=	337.5 g
1 lb	=	450 g
1.5 lb	=	675 g

Cups to Grams (g)

1 cup flour or icing sugar	=	125 g
1 cup butter	=	225 g
1 cup sugar	=	200 g

Note: *Remember that the weight of grams can change based on the specific dry ingredient being used.*

Fluid Ounces (fl oz) to Millilitres (ml)

1 fl oz	=	30 ml
2 fl oz	=	60 ml
3 fl oz	=	90 ml
4 fl oz	=	120 ml
5 fl oz	=	150 ml

Cups to Milliliters (ml)

¼ lb	=	59 ml
½ lb	=	118 ml
1 lb	=	236 ml
1.5 lb	=	354 ml

Others

US teaspoon	=	5 ml
US dessert spoon	=	10 ml
US tablespoon	=	17.7 ml
1 US pint	=	473 ml
1 quart	=	946 ml
1/2 Butter stick	=	56 g
1 Butter stick		113 g

CHAPTER 1
BREAKFAST RECIPES

Breakfast Egg Bites

Cook time: 25 minutes
Serves: 12
Per Serving: Calories 201, Carbs 0.5g,
Fat 15g, Protein 14g

Ingredients:

- Eggs - 6
- Egg whites - 1 cup
- Ground pork sausage - 1 lb
- Mozzarella cheese - 1/2 cup
- Cheddar cheese - 1 cup
- Paprika - 1/4 tsp
- Pepper
- Salt

Directions:

1. Brown sausage in a pan over medium-high heat.
2. Divide cheese and cooked sausages into silicone muffin molds.
3. In a large bowl, whisk together egg whites, egg, paprika, pepper, and salt.
4. Pour egg mixture into each muffin mold.
5. Place a crisper plate in both baskets.
6. Place muffin molds in both baskets, then insert baskets in the unit.
7. Press zone 1, then select bake mode.
8. Set the temperature to 350 F/ 180 C and time to 25 minutes.
9. Press MATCH mode, then press start.
10. Serve and enjoy.

Spinach Egg Cups

Cook time: 20 minutes
Serves: 6
Per Serving: Calories 135, Carbs 0.7g,
Fat 11g, Protein 7g

Ingredients:

- Eggs - 4
- Ground sausage - 1/4 lb
- Fresh spinach - 1 cup
- Baking powder - 1/4 tsp
- Olive oil - 1 tbsp
- Unsweetened almond milk - 1 ½ tbsp20
- Pepper
- Salt

Directions:

1. Heat oil in a pan over medium heat.
2. Add sausage to the pan and cook until lightly brown.
3. Whisk eggs with baking powder, milk, pepper, and salt in a bowl.
4. Add sausage and spinach and stir until well combined.
5. Divide egg mixture into silicone muffin molds.
6. Place a crisper plate in both baskets.
7. Place muffin molds in both baskets, then insert baskets in the unit.
8. Press zone 1, then select bake mode.
9. Set the temperature to 375 F/ 190 C and time to 20 minutes.
10. Press MATCH mode, then press start.
11. Serve and enjoy.

Healthy Sweet Potato Hash

Cook time: 25 minutes
Serves: 4
Per Serving: Calories 201, Carbs 35g,
Fat 5g, Protein 6g

Ingredients:

- Large sweet potato peeled and cubed - 1
- Chickpeas, drained - 15 oz can
- Paprika - 1 tsp
- Garlic powder - 1 tsp
- Olive oil - 1 tbsp
- Bell pepper, chopped - 1
- Onion, diced - 1
- Pepper
- Salt

Directions:

1. Add sweet potato, bell pepper, chickpeas, and remaining ingredients into the mixing bowl and toss well.
2. Place a crisper plate in both baskets.
3. Add sweet potato mixture in both baskets, then insert baskets in the unit.
4. Press zone 1, then select air fry mode.
5. Set the temperature to 350 F/ 180 C and time to 25 minutes.
6. Press MATCH mode, then press start.
7. Serve and enjoy.

Apple Oatmeal Cups

Cook time: 20 minutes
Serves: 6
Per Serving: Calories 140, Carbs 26g,
Fat 2g, Protein 5g

Ingredients:

- Egg - 1
- Apple, diced - 1/2
- Honey - 2 tbsp
- Quick oats - 1 1/2 cups
- Applesauce - 1/2 cup
- Unsweetened almond milk - 1/2 cup
- Cinnamon - 1 tsp
- Baking powder - 3/4 tsp

Directions:

1. Add all ingredients into the mixing bowl and mix until well combined.
2. Spoon batter into silicone muffin molds.
3. Place a crisper plate in both baskets.
4. Place muffin molds in both baskets, then insert baskets in the unit.
5. Press zone 1, then select bake mode.
6. Set the temperature to 375 F/ 190 C and time to 20 minutes.
7. Press MATCH mode, then press start.
8. Serve and enjoy.

Delicious Quiche Cups

Cook time: 20 minutes
Serves: 12
Per Serving: Calories 76, Carbs 1.6g,
Fat 5.4g, Protein 6.2g

Ingredients:

- Eggs - 8
- Bell pepper, diced - 1/4 cup
- Cheddar cheese, shredded - 3/4 cup
- Frozen spinach, chopped - 10 oz
- Onion, chopped - 1/4 cup
- Mushroom, diced - 1/4 cup
- Pepper
- Salt

Directions:

1. In a bowl, whisk eggs with pepper and salt.
2. Add bell pepper, cheese, spinach, onion, and mushroom, and stir well to combine.
3. Pour the egg mixture into the silicone muffin molds.
4. Place a crisper plate in both baskets.
5. Place muffin molds in both baskets, then insert baskets in the unit.
6. Press zone 1, then select bake mode.
7. Set the temperature to 375 F/ 190 C and the time to 20 minutes.
8. Press MATCH mode, then press start.
9. Serve and enjoy.

Cinnamon Sweet Potato Muffins

Cook time: 25 minutes
Serves: 12
Per Serving: Calories 105, Carbs 22g,
Fat 0.5g, Protein 2.6g

Ingredients:

- Sweet potatoes, cooked and mashed - 2 1/2 cups
- Ground cinnamon - 1 tsp
- Baking powder - 3 tsp
- Unsweetened almond milk - 3/4 cup
- Coconut sugar - 1/2 cup
- Whole wheat flour - 1 1/2 cups
- Vanilla - 1/2 tsp
- Pinch of salt

Directions:

1. Add mashed sweet potatoes, milk, and vanilla to the blender and blend until smooth.
2. Mix flour, coconut sugar, cinnamon, baking powder, and salt in a large bowl.
3. Add sweet potato mixture and mix until well combined.
4. Spoon batter into the silicone muffin molds.
5. Place a crisper plate in both baskets.
6. Place muffin molds in both baskets, then insert baskets in the unit.
7. Press zone 1, then select bake mode.
8. Set the temperature to 350 F/ 180 C and time to 25 minutes.
9. Press MATCH mode, then press start.
10. Serve and enjoy.

Sweet Potato Bell Pepper Hash

Cook time: 15 minutes
Serves: 4
Per Serving: Calories 215, Carbs 36g,
Fat 7.4g, Protein 2.4g

Ingredients:

- Large sweet potatoes, peel & cut into 1/2-inch pieces - 3
- Olive oil - 2 tbsp
- Bell pepper cut into 1/2-inch pieces - 1
- Medium onion, cut into 1/2-inch pieces - 1
- Dried thyme - 1/2 tsp
- Nutmeg - 1/2 tsp
- Cinnamon - 1/2 tsp
- Pepper
- Salt

Directions:

1. In a bowl, toss sweet potatoes with the remaining ingredients.
2. Place a crisper plate in both baskets.
3. Add sweet potato mixture in both baskets, then insert baskets in the unit.
4. Press zone 1, then select air fry mode.
5. Set the temperature to 350 F/ 180 C and the time to 15 minutes.
6. Press MATCH mode, then press start.
7. Serve and enjoy.

Oatmeal Chocó Chip Muffins

Cook time: 20 minutes
Serves: 8
Per Serving: Calories 440, Carbs 50g,
Fat 21g, Protein 14g

Ingredients:

- Egg - 1
- Quick oats - 1 cup
- Flour - 1 1/2 cups
- Greek yogurt - 1 cup
- Baking soda - 1/2 tsp
- Baking powder - 1 tsp
- Brown sugar - 1/2 cup
- Chocolate chips - 1/4 cup
- Vanilla - 1 tbsp
- Peanut butter - 3/4 cup
- Milk - 1/4 cup
- Butter, melted - 1/4 cup
- Bananas, mashed - 2

Directions:

1. Mix flour, baking soda, baking powder, chocolate chips, sugar, and oats in a bowl.
2. Mix egg, peanut butter, milk, vanilla, butter, bananas, and yogurt in a separate bowl.
3. Add flour mixture into the egg mixture and mix until well combined.
4. Spoon batter into the silicone muffin molds.
5. Place a crisper plate in both baskets.
6. Place muffin molds in both baskets, then insert baskets in the unit.
7. Press zone 1, then select air fry mode.
8. Set the temperature to 375 F/ 190 C and time to 20 minutes.
9. Press MATCH mode, then press start.
10. Serve and enjoy.

Cinnamon Apple French Toast

Cook time: 10 minutes
Serves: 8
Per Serving: Calories 54, Carbs 10g,
Fat 0.9g, Protein 1.5g

Ingredients:

- Egg, lightly beaten - 1
- Bread slices - 8
- Cinnamon - 1 1/2 tbsp
- Milk - 1 tbsp
- Maple syrup - 2 tbsp
- Applesauce - 6 tbsp

Directions:

1. Mix egg, applesauce, milk, cinnamon, and maple syrup in a bowl.
2. Place a crisper plate in both baskets.
3. Dip each bread slice in egg mixture, place in both baskets, then insert baskets in the unit.
4. Press zone 1, then select air fry mode.
5. Set the temperature to 350 F/ 180 C and time to 10 minutes.
6. Press MATCH mode, then press start.
7. Serve and enjoy.

Parmesan Garlic Bread

Cook time: 5 minutes
Serves: 4
Per Serving: Calories 245, Carbs 13g,
Fat 17g, Protein 10g

Ingredients:

- Baguette cut into 4/5-inch-thick slices - 1
- Oregano - 1 tsp
- Butter, melted - 1/4 cup
- Milk - 1/4 cup
- Fresh parsley, chopped - 1/4 cup
- Parmesan cheese, grated - 1 cup
- Garlic cloves, minced - 8
- Red pepper flakes, crushed - 1 tsp

Directions:

1. Mix butter, parsley, milk, red pepper flakes, oregano, and garlic in a small bowl.
2. Brush one side of each baguette slice with butter mixture and top with grated cheese.
3. Place a crisper plate in both baskets.
4. Place baguette slices in both baskets, then insert baskets in the unit.
5. Press zone 1, then select air fry mode.
6. Set the temperature to 350 F/ 180 C and time to 5 minutes.
7. Press MATCH mode, then press start.
8. Serve and enjoy.

CHAPTER 2
LUNCH RECIPES

BAKED BRUSSELS SPROUT & BROCCOLI

BAKED MIXED VEGETABLES

SPICY LAMB SHOULDER

FISH ZUCCHINI PEPPER SKEWERS

MAPLE GARLIC SALMON

EASY CAJUN SHRIMP

TASTY BEEF KABABS

FLAVORS LAMB PATTIES

MEAT RICE STUFFED PEPPERS

PARMESAN CHICKEN BREAST

Baked Brussels Sprout & Broccoli

Cook time: 30 minutes
Serves: 6
Per Serving: Calories 123, Carbs 13g,
Fat 7.3g, Protein 5.7g

Ingredients:
- Brussels sprouts, cut ends - 1 lb
- Broccoli, cut into florets - 1 lb
- Olive oil - 3 tbsp
- Onion, chopped - 1/2
- Paprika - 1 tsp
- Garlic powder - 1 tsp
- Pepper - 1/2 tsp
- Salt - 3/4 tsp

Directions:
1. Add all ingredients into the bowl and toss well.
2. Place a crisper plate in both baskets.
3. Add vegetable mixture in both baskets, then insert baskets in the unit.
4. Press zone 1, then select bake mode.
5. Set the temperature to 388 F/ 198 C and the time to 30 minutes.
6. Press MATCH mode, then press start.
7. Serve and enjoy.

Baked Mixed Vegetables

Cook time: 35 minutes
Serves: 4
Per Serving: Calories 196, Carbs 18g,
Fat 13g, Protein 6.5g

Ingredients:
- Zucchini cut into 1/2-inch-thick half circles - 2
- Brussels sprouts, cut in half - 3 cups
- Bell peppers, cut into 2-inch chunks - 2
- Mushrooms, cut in half - 8 oz
- Onion, cut into wedges - 1
- Vinegar - 2 tbsp
- Thyme - 1 tsp
- Olive oil - 1/4 cup
- Salt - 1/2 tsp

Directions:
1. Add all vegetables and remaining ingredients into the mixing bowl and toss well. Cover and place in refrigerator for 1 hour to marinate.
2. Place a crisper plate in both baskets.
3. Add marinated vegetables in both baskets, then insert baskets in the unit.
4. Press zone 1, then select bake mode.
5. Set the temperature to 375 F/ 190 C and the time to 35 minutes.
6. Press MATCH mode, then press start.
7. Serve and enjoy.

Spicy Lamb Shoulder

Cook time: 15 minutes
Serves: 6
Per Serving: Calories 264, Carbs 2.6g,
Fat 10g, Protein 37g

Ingredients:

- Lamb shoulder, boneless & cut into pieces - 2 lbs

For spice mixture:

- Ground fennel - 1 tsp
- Sesame seeds - 1 tbsp
- Chili powder - 1 tbsp
- Peppercorns - 1/8 tsp
- Cumin seeds - 1 tsp
- Garlic powder - 1 tsp
- Ground ginger - 1 tsp
- Cumin powder - 2 tbsp
- Pepper
- Salt

Directions:

1. In a small bowl, mix all spice mixture ingredients.
2. In a mixing bowl, add meat and spice mixture and mix until meat is well coated.
3. Place a crisper plate in both baskets.
4. Add meat in both baskets, then insert baskets in the unit.
5. Press zone 1, then select air fry mode.
6. Set the temperature to 350 F/ 180 C and time to 15 minutes.
7. Press MATCH mode, then press start.
8. Serve and enjoy.

Fish Zucchini Pepper Skewers

Cook time: 10 minutes
Serves: 4
Per Serving: Calories 140, Carbs 15g,
Fat 3g, Protein 16g

Ingredients:

- Swordfish steak, cut into small chunks - 2
- Bell pepper, cut into pieces - 2
- Zucchini, cut into pieces - 2
- Lemon, cut into slices - 2
- Onion, cut into pieces - 2
- Pepper
- Salt

Directions:

1. Season fish chunks with pepper and salt.
2. Thread fish chunks, onion, bell pepper, and zucchini pieces onto the soaked skewers.
3. Place a crisper plate in both baskets.
4. Arrange lemon slices in both baskets, then place skewers on lemon slices. Insert baskets in the unit.
5. Press zone 1, then select air fry mode.
6. Set the temperature to 375 F/ 190 C and time to 10 minutes.
7. Press MATCH mode, then press start.
8. Serve and enjoy.

Maple Garlic Salmon

Cook time: 8 minutes
Serves: 4
Per Serving: Calories 280, Carbs 11g,
Fat 11g, Protein 35g

Ingredients:

- Salmon fillets - 4
- Soy sauce - 3 tbsp
- Maple syrup - 3 tbsp
- Garlic clove, minced - 2
- Sriracha hot sauce - 1 tbsp

Directions:

1. Coat salmon fillets with soy sauce, garlic, hot sauce, and maple syrup.
2. Place a crisper plate in both baskets.
3. Place salmon fillets in both baskets, then insert baskets in the unit.
4. Press zone 1, then select air fry mode.
5. Set the temperature to 392 F/ 200 C and time to 8 minutes.
6. Press MATCH mode, then press start.
7. Serve and enjoy.

Easy Cajun Shrimp

Cook time: 8 minutes
Serves: 4
Per Serving: Calories 365, Carbs 7g,
Fat 21g, Protein 35g

Ingredients:

- Shrimp, peeled and deveined - 1 lb
- Yellow squash, sliced - 1
- Zucchini, sliced - 1
- Sausage, sliced - 6 oz
- Cajun seasoning - 1 tbsp
- Olive oil - 2 tbsp
- Bell pepper, cut into 1-inch pieces - 1
- Pepper
- Salt

Directions:

1. Toss shrimp, zucchini, oil, Cajun seasoning, bell pepper, squash, sausage, pepper, and salt in a bowl.
2. Place a crisper plate in both baskets.
3. Divide the shrimp mixture into both baskets, then insert baskets in the unit.
4. Press zone 1, then select air fry mode.
5. Set the temperature to 392 F/ 200 C and time to 8 minutes.
6. Press MATCH mode, then press start.
7. Serve and enjoy.

Tasty Beef Kababs

Cook time: 10 minutes
Serves: 4
Per Serving: Calories 215, Carbs 4g,
Fat 8g, Protein 28g

Ingredients:

- Beef ribs, cut into 1-inch pieces - 1 lb
- Bell pepper, cut into pieces - 1
- Soy sauce - 2 tbsp
- Onion, cut into pieces - 1/2
- Sour cream - 1/3 cup
- Pepper
- Salt

Directions:

1. Mix meat, soy sauce, onion, bell pepper, sour cream, pepper, and salt in a bowl. Cover and place in refrigerator for 1 hour to marinate.
2. Thread marinated meat, onion, and bell pepper pieces onto the soaked skewers.
3. Place a crisper plate in both baskets.
4. Place skewers in both baskets, then insert baskets in the unit.
5. Press zone 1, then select air fry mode.
6. Set the temperature to 392 F/ 200 C and the time to 10 minutes.
7. Press MATCH mode, then press start.
8. Serve and enjoy.

Flavors Lamb Patties

Cook time: 12 minutes
Serves: 8
Per Serving: Calories 215, Carbs 0.8g,
Fat 8.8g, Protein 32g

Ingredients:

- Ground lamb - 2 lbs
- Ground coriander - 1 tbsp
- Fresh parsley, chopped - 2 tbsp
- Garlic, minced - 1 tsp
- Cinnamon - 1/2 tsp
- Paprika - 1 tsp
- Ground cumin - 1 tbsp
- Pepper
- Salt

Directions:

1. Add meat and remaining ingredients into the mixing bowl until well combined.
2. Place a crisper plate in both baskets.
3. Make patties from the meat mixture and place them in both baskets, then insert baskets in the unit.
4. Press zone 1, then select bake mode.
5. Set the temperature to 392 F/ 200 C and time to 12 minutes.
6. Press MATCH mode, then press start.
7. Serve and enjoy.

Meat Rice Stuffed Peppers

Cook time: 15 minutes
Serves: 8
Per Serving: Calories 445, Carbs 50g,
Fat 8g, Protein 39g

Ingredients:

- Bell peppers, cut top & remove seeds - 8
- Ground beef - 2 lbs
- Tomato sauce - 2 cups
- Cooked rice - 2 cups
- Onion powder - 1 tsp
- Italian seasoning - 2 tbsp
- Worcestershire sauce - 2 tbsp
- Pepper
- Salt

Directions:

1. Mix ground beef, Italian seasoning, onion powder, rice, tomato sauce, Worcestershire sauce, pepper, and salt in a bowl.
2. Stuff the meat mixture into each bell pepper.
3. Place a crisper plate in both baskets.
4. Place stuffed bell peppers in both baskets, then insert baskets in the unit.
5. Press zone 1, then select bake mode.
6. Set the temperature to 350 F/ 180 C and the time to 15 minutes.
7. Press MATCH mode, then press start.
8. Serve and enjoy.

Parmesan Chicken Breast

Cook time: 14 minutes
Serves: 4
Per Serving: Calories 246, Carbs 2.8g,
Fat 11.1g, Protein 33g

Ingredients:

- Eggs, lightly beaten - 2
- Chicken breast, boneless - 16 oz
- Parmesan cheese, grated - 3/4 cup
- Almond flour - 3/4 cup
- Dill pickle juice - 3/4 cup
- Pepper
- Salt

Directions:

1. Add chicken and dill pickle juice in a bowl and mix well. Cover and place in refrigerator for 2 hours to marinate.
2. Mix almond flour, parmesan cheese, pepper, and salt in a shallow dish.
3. In a separate shallow bowl, whisk eggs with pepper and salt.
4. Remove the chicken from the marinade.
5. Dip each chicken breast in egg, then coat with almond flour mixture.
6. Place a crisper plate in both baskets.
7. Place coated chicken in both baskets, then insert baskets in the unit.
8. Press zone 1, then select air fry mode.
9. Set the temperature to 392 F/ 200 C and time to 14 minutes.
10. Press MATCH mode, then press start.
11. Serve and enjoy.

CHAPTER 3
Appetizers
And
Side Dishes

Cauliflower Cheese Patties

Cook time: 10 minutes
Serves: 4
Per Serving: Calories 166, Carbs 11.8g,
Fat 8g, Protein 10.5g

Ingredients:

- Eggs - 2
- Cauliflower rice, microwave for 5 minutes - 2 cups
- Cheddar cheese, shredded - 1/2 cup
- Breadcrumbs - 1/3 cup
- Mozzarella cheese, shredded - 1/2 cup
- Dried basil - 1 tsp
- Garlic powder - 1 tsp
- Onion powder - 1/2 tsp
- Pepper
- Salt

Directions:

1. Add cauliflower rice and remaining ingredients into the mixing bowl and mix until well combined.
2. Place a crisper plate in both baskets.
3. Make patties from the cauliflower mixture, place them in both baskets, then insert baskets in the unit.
4. Press zone 1, then select air fry mode.
5. Set the temperature to 392 F/ 200 C and the time to 10 minutes.
6. Press MATCH mode, then press start.
7. Serve and enjoy.

Easy Bread Pizza

Cook time: 8 minutes
Serves: 4
Per Serving: Calories 132, Carbs 17g,
Fat 4.3g, Protein 7.3g

Ingredients:

- French Bread loaf, cut in half lengthwise - 1
- Mozzarella cheese, shredded - 1 cup
- Olives, sliced - 1/4 cup
- Pizza sauce - 1 cup
- Mozzarella cheese, shredded - 1 cup
- Basil leaves - 6
- Pepper
- Salt

Directions:

1. Spread sauce on the cut side of each bread slice.
2. Add mozzarella cheese, parmesan cheese, olives, basil, pepper, and salt on top of the bread slices.
3. Place a crisper plate in both baskets.
4. Place bread slices in both baskets, then insert baskets in the unit.
5. Press zone 1, then select air fry mode.
6. Set the temperature to 350 F/ 180 C and time to 8 minutes.
7. Press MATCH mode, then press start.
8. Serve and enjoy.

Crispy Potato Fries

Cook time: 20 minutes
Serves: 6
Per Serving: Calories 75, Carbs 12g,
Fat 2.3g, Protein 1.4g

Ingredients:

- Potatoes, cut into fries' shape - 1 lb
- Steak seasoning - 1/2 tsp
- Paprika - 1/2 tbsp
- Garlic powder - 1 tsp
- Olive oil - 1 tbsp
- Pepper
- Salt

Directions:

1. Toss potato fries with steak seasoning, garlic powder, oil, paprika, pepper, and salt in a bowl.
2. Place a crisper plate in both baskets.
3. Add potato fries in both baskets, then insert baskets in the unit.
4. Press zone 1, then select air fry mode.
5. Set the temperature to 392 F/ 200 C and time to 20 minutes.
6. Press MATCH mode, then press start.
7. Serve and enjoy.

Parmesan Baby Potatoes

Cook time: 15 minutes
Serves: 4
Per Serving: Calories 165, Carbs 15.1g,
Fat 9.4g, Protein 6.1g

Ingredients:

- Baby potatoes rinse & pat dry - 1 lb
- Dried basil - 1/2 tsp
- Paprika - 1/2 tsp
- Garlic powder - 1 1/2 tsp
- Parsley, chopped - 2 tbsp
- Parmesan cheese, grated - 1/2 cup
- Olive oil - 2 tbsp
- Pepper
- Salt

Directions:

1. In a bowl, toss potatoes with the remaining ingredients until well coated.
2. Place a crisper plate in both baskets.
3. Add potatoes in both baskets, then insert baskets in the unit.
4. Press zone 1, then select air fry mode.
5. Set the temperature to 392 F/ 200 C and time to 15 minutes.
6. Press MATCH mode, then press start.
7. Serve and enjoy.

Candied Cinnamon Walnuts

Cook time: 10 minutes
Serves: 16
Per Serving: Calories 215, Carbs 4.2g,
Fat 19.4g, Protein 7.4g

Ingredients:
- Walnuts, halved - 4 cups
- Butter, melted - 2 tbsp
- Cinnamon - 1/2 tsp
- Brown sugar - 3 tbsp
- Vanilla - 1 1/2 tsp
- Salt

Directions:
1. Toss walnuts with brown sugar, butter, vanilla, cinnamon, and salt in a bowl.
2. Place a crisper plate in both baskets.
3. Add walnuts in both baskets, then insert baskets in the unit.
4. Press zone 1, then select air fry mode.
5. Set the temperature to 392 F/ 200 C and time to 10 minutes.
6. Press MATCH mode, then press start.
7. Serve and enjoy.

Flavors Crab Cake Poppers

Cook time: 10 minutes
Serves: 6
Per Serving: Calories 219, Carbs 7g,
Fat 20.2g, Protein 17.2g

Ingredients:
- Egg, lightly beaten - 1
- Lump crab meat drained - 16 oz
- Garlic, minced - 1 tsp
- Lemon juice - 1 tsp
- Old Bay seasoning - 1 tsp
- Almond flour - 5 tbsp
- Dijon mustard - 1 tsp
- Mayonnaise - 2 tbsp
- Pepper
- Salt

Directions:
1. In a bowl, mix crab meat and remaining ingredients until well combined.
2. Place small balls from the crab meat mixture on a plate.
3. Place the plate in the refrigerator for 60 minutes.
4. Place a crisper plate in both baskets.
5. Place prepared crab meat balls in both baskets, then insert baskets in the unit.
6. Press zone 1, then select air fry mode.
7. Set the temperature to 350 F/ 180 C and time to 10 minutes.
8. Press MATCH mode, then press start.
9. Serve and enjoy.

Tasty Potato Tots

Cook time: 15 minutes
Serves: 4
Per Serving: Calories 340, Carbs 38.3g,
Fat 14.6g, Protein 14.1g

Ingredients:

- Potatoes, peeled, boiled, & grated - 4
- Cheddar cheese, grated - 1 1/2 cups
- All-purpose flour - 3 tbsp
- Paprika - 1/4 tsp
- Pepper
- Salt

Directions:

1. Mix grated potatoes, cheese, flour, paprika, pepper, and salt in a bowl until well combined.
2. Place a crisper plate in both baskets.
3. Make small tots from the potato mixture and place them in both baskets, then insert baskets into the unit.
4. Press zone 1, then select air fry mode.
5. Set the temperature to 375 F/ 190 C and time to 15 minutes.
6. Press MATCH mode, then press start.
7. Serve and enjoy.

Chicken Spinach Cheese Bites

Cook time: 12 minutes
Serves: 4
Per Serving: Calories 275, Carbs 1.5g,
Fat 11.7g, Protein 39.9g

Ingredients:

- Ground chicken - 1 lb
- Onion powder - 1/4 tsp
- Cottage cheese - 1/3 cup
- Baby spinach, chopped - 1/3 cup
- Feta cheese, crumbled - 1 oz
- Ground pork rinds - 1/2 oz
- Garlic powder - 1/2 tsp
- Pepper
- Salt

Directions:

1. Add chicken and remaining ingredients into the mixing bowl until well combined.
2. Place a crisper plate in both baskets.
3. Make small balls from the chicken mixture and place them in both baskets, then insert baskets in the unit.
4. Press zone 1, then select air fry mode.
5. Set the temperature to 350 F/ 180 C and time to 12 minutes.
6. Press MATCH mode, then press start.
7. Serve and enjoy.

Crispy Squash Fritters

Cook time: 15 minutes
Serves: 6
Per Serving: Calories 206, Carbs 38g,
Fat 3.2g, Protein 9.1g

Ingredients:

- Egg, lightly beaten - 1
- Butternut squash, grated - 6 cups
- Chickpea flour - 1 cup
- Garlic cloves, minced - 3
- Onion, sliced - 1 small
- Ground cumin - 1 1/2 tsp
- Parsley chopped - 1/2 cup
- Pepper
- Salt

Directions:

1. Mix butternut squash and remaining ingredients in a mixing bowl until well combined.
2. Place a crisper plate in both baskets.
3. Make small patties from the butternut squash mixture and place them in both baskets, then insert baskets in the unit.
4. Press zone 1, then select air fry mode.
5. Set the temperature to 375 F/ 190 C and time to 15 minutes.
6. Press MATCH mode, then press start.
7. Serve and enjoy.

Cinnamon Apple Slices

Cook time: 8 minutes
Serves: 4
Per Serving: Calories 60, Carbs 15g,
Fat 0.2g, Protein 0.3g

Ingredients:

- Apples, cored and cut into 1/8-inch-thick slices - 2
- Powdered sugar - 1/2 tbsp
- Cinnamon - 1 tsp

Directions:

1. In a small bowl, mix cinnamon and sugar and set aside.
2. Place a crisper plate in both baskets.
3. Arrange apple slices in both baskets, then sprinkle with cinnamon sugar mixture. Insert baskets in the unit.
4. Press zone 1, then select dehydrate mode.
5. Set the temperature to 140 F/ 60 C and time to 8 hours.
6. Press MATCH mode, then press start.

CHAPTER 4

FISH AND SEAFOOD RECIPES

BAKED PARMESAN TILAPIA

SALMON VEGGIE PATTIES

QUICK SHRIMP SKEWERS

LEMON PEPPER BASA

SOUTHWESTERN TROUT FILLETS

CRISPY BREADED FISH FILLETS

TUNA PATTIES

PARMESAN GARLIC SHRIMP

DELICIOUS FISH CAKES

SPICY SHRIMP

Baked Parmesan Tilapia

Cook time: 20 minutes
Serves: 6
Per Serving: Calories 194, Carbs 5.2g,
Fat 9.2g, Protein 23.7g

Ingredients:

- Tilapia fillets - 6
- Parmesan cheese, grated - 1/2 cup
- Garlic, crushed - 1 tsp
- Mayonnaise - 1/2 cup
- Dried basil - 1/4 tsp
- Dried thyme - 1/4 tsp
- Pepper
- Salt

Directions:

1. Place a crisper plate in both baskets. Line both baskets with parchment paper.
2. Arrange fish fillets in both baskets.
3. Mix parmesan cheese, mayonnaise, basil, thyme, garlic, pepper, and salt in a small bowl.
4. Spread cheese mixture on top of fish fillets. Insert baskets in the unit.
5. Press zone 1, then select bake mode.
6. Set the temperature to 350 F/ 180 C and time to 20 minutes.
7. Press MATCH mode, then press start.
8. Serve and enjoy.

Salmon Veggie Patties

Cook time: 15 minutes
Serves: 8
Per Serving: Calories 159, Carbs 12.1g,
Fat 71g, Protein 14.8g

Ingredients:

- Eggs, lightly beaten - 2
- Salmon, drained & flaked - 15 oz can
- Chives, chopped - 1/4 cup
- Parsley, chopped - 2 tbsp
- Carrot, grated - 1
- All-purpose flour - 1/4 cup
- Breadcrumbs - 3/4 cup
- Zucchini, grated - 1
- Pepper
- Salt

Directions:

1. Add fish and remaining ingredients in a bowl and mix until well combined.
2. Place a crisper plate in both baskets.
3. Make patties from the fish mixture and place them in both baskets, then insert baskets in the unit.
4. Press zone 1, then select air fry mode.
5. Set the temperature to 392 F/ 200 C and time to 15 minutes.
6. Press MATCH mode, then press start.
7. Serve and enjoy.

Quick Shrimp Skewers

Cook time: 8 minutes
Serves: 8
Per Serving: Calories 119, Carbs 3.2g,
Fat 3.2g, Protein 14.7g

Ingredients:

- Shrimp, peeled & deveined - 1 lb
- Fresh lemon juice - 1/2 tbsp
- Soy sauce, low-sodium - 1 tbsp
- Olive oil - 1/2 tbsp
- Sriracha - 1 tbsp
- Honey - 1 tbsp
- Garlic, minced - 1/2 tsp

Directions:

1. In a bowl, toss shrimp with the remaining ingredients until well-coated.
2. Cover bowl and set aside for 1 hour.
3. Thread shrimp onto the soaked skewers.
4. Place a crisper plate in both baskets.
5. Place shrimp skewers in both baskets, then insert baskets in the unit.
6. Press zone 1, then select air fry mode.
7. Set the temperature to 350 F/ 180 C and the time to 8 minutes.
8. Press MATCH mode, then press start.
9. Serve and enjoy.

Lemon Pepper Basa

Cook time: 15 minutes
Serves: 4
Per Serving: Calories 308, Carbs 5.5g,
Fat 21.4g, Protein 24.1g

Ingredients:

- Basa fish fillets - 4
- Fresh parsley, chopped - 2 tbsp
- Green onion, sliced - 1/4 cup
- Garlic powder - 1/2 tsp
- Lemon pepper seasoning - 1/4 tsp
- Fresh lemon juice - 4 tbsp
- Olive oil - 8 tsp
- Pepper
- Salt

Directions:

1. Place a crisper plate in both baskets.
2. Place fish fillets in both baskets. Brush fish fillets with lemon juice and oil.
3. Sprinkle lemon pepper seasoning, garlic powder, green onion, parsley, pepper, and salt over fish fillets. Insert baskets in the unit.
4. Press zone 1, then select bake mode.
5. Set the temperature to 392 F/ 200 C and time to 15 minutes.
6. Press MATCH mode, then press start.
7. Serve and enjoy.

Southwestern Trout Fillets

Cook time: 16 minutes
Serves: 4
Per Serving: Calories 272, Carbs 5g,
Fat 13.5g, Protein 31.1g

Ingredients:

- Trout fillets - 1 lb
- Garlic powder - 1 tsp
- Breadcrumbs - 3 tbsp
- Olive oil - 1 tbsp
- Chili powder - 1 tsp
- Onion powder - 1 tsp
- Pepper
- Salt

Directions:

1. Mix breadcrumbs, onion powder, garlic powder, chili powder, pepper, and salt in a small bowl.
2. Brush fish fillets with oil and coat them with breadcrumbs.
3. Place a crisper plate in both baskets.
4. Place coated fish fillets in both baskets, then insert baskets in the unit.
5. Press zone 1, then select air fry mode.
6. Set the temperature to 375 F/ 190 C and time to 1(minutes.
7. Press MATCH mode, then press start.
8. Serve and enjoy.

Crispy Breaded Fish Fillets

Cook time: 10 minutes
Serves: 4
Per Serving: Calories 397, Carbs 53g,
Fat 6.2g, Protein 31g

Ingredients:

- Eggs - 2
- Cod fillets - 4
- Sweet paprika - 1/2 tsp
- All-purpose flour - 1/4 cup
- Garlic powder - 1/2 tsp
- Onion powder - 1/2 tsp
- Breadcrumbs - 2 cups
- Tabasco - 1 tbsp
- Water - 2 tbsp
- Cornstarch - 1/4 cup
- Pepper
- Salt

Directions:

1. Mix flour, onion powder, paprika, garlic powder, cornstarch, pepper, and salt in a shallow dish.
2. In a separate shallow dish, whisk egg, tabasco, and water.
3. Mix breadcrumbs, pepper, sweet paprika, and salt in a third shallow dish.
4. Coat each fish fillet with flour, dip in egg, and coat with breadcrumbs.
5. Place a crisper plate in both baskets.
6. Place coated fish fillets in both baskets, then insert baskets in the unit.
7. Press zone 1, then select air fry mode.
8. Set the temperature to 392 F/ 200 C and time to 10 minutes.
9. Press MATCH mode, then press start.
10. Serve and enjoy.

Tuna Patties

Cook time: 10 minutes
Serves: 10
Per Serving: Calories 99, Carbs 5.2g,
Fat 2.3g, Protein 14g

Ingredients:

- Eggs - 2
- Tuna, drained & diced - 15 oz can
- Garlic powder - 1/2 tsp
- Onion, minced - 3 tbsp
- Celery stalk, chopped - 1
- Parmesan cheese, grated - 3 tbsp
- Dried oregano - 1/2 tsp
- Dried basil - 1/2 tsp
- Dried thyme - 1/2 tsp
- Breadcrumbs - 1/2 cup
- Lemon juice - 1 tbsp
- Lemon zest - 1
- Pepper
- Salt

Directions:

1. In a mixing bowl, add tuna and remaining ingredients and mix until well combined.
2. Place a crisper plate in both baskets.
3. Make patties from tuna mixture and place them in both baskets, then insert baskets in the unit.
4. Press zone 1, then select air fry mode.
5. Set the temperature to 350 F/ 180 C and time to 10 minutes.
6. Press MATCH mode, then press start.
7. Serve and enjoy.

Parmesan Garlic Shrimp

Cook time: 10 minutes
Serves: 6
Per Serving: Calories 256, Carbs 3.5g,
Fat 9.4g, Protein 37.8g

Ingredients:

- Cooked shrimp, peeled & deveined - 2 lbs
- Oregano - 1/2 tsp
- Parmesan cheese, grated - 2/3 cup
- Garlic, minced - 1 tbsp
- Olive oil - 2 tbsp
- Onion powder - 1 tsp
- Basil - 1 tsp
- Pepper
- Salt

Directions:

1. Toss shrimp with oregano, cheese, garlic, oil, onion powder, basil, pepper, and salt in a bowl.
2. Place a crisper plate in both baskets.
3. Add shrimp mixture in both baskets, then insert baskets in the unit.
4. Press zone 1, then select air fry mode.
5. Set the temperature to 350 F/ 180 C and time to 10 minutes.
6. Press MATCH mode, then press start.
7. Serve and enjoy.

Delicious Fish Cakes

Cook time: 10 minutes
Serves: 8
Per Serving: Calories 177, Carbs 11.4g,
Fat 9.2g, Protein 11.7g

Ingredients:

- Egg - 1
- Cooked crawfish meat - 1 lb
- Worcestershire sauce - 1 tbsp
- Dijon mustard - 1 tbsp
- Hot sauce - 1 tsp
- Crackers, crushed - 1 1/2 cup
- Bell pepper, minced - 1/4 cup
- Parsley, chopped - 1 tsp
- Mayonnaise - 1/2 cup
- Pepper
- Salt

Directions:

1. Mix cooked fish meat with the remaining ingredients in a bowl until well combined.
2. Place a crisper plate in both baskets.
3. Make patties from the fish meat mixture and place them in both baskets, then insert baskets in the unit.
4. Press zone 1, then select air fry mode.
5. Set the temperature to 350 F/ 180 C and time to 10 minutes.
6. Press MATCH mode, then press start.
7. Serve and enjoy.

Spicy Shrimp

Cook time: 10 minutes
Serves: 4
Per Serving: Calories 290, Carbs 7.5g,
Fat 4.2g, Protein 52.1g

Ingredients:

- Shrimp, peeled & deveined - 2 lbs
- Ground cumin - 1 tsp
- Liquid smoke - 1 tsp
- Chili powder - 1 tsp
- Fresh lemon juice - 1 tbsp
- Worcestershire sauce - 2 tbsp
- Garlic powder - 1 tsp
- Sugar - 1 tsp
- Tabasco sauce - 1 tsp
- Smoked paprika - 1 tsp
- Pepper
- Salt

Directions:

1. In a bowl, toss shrimp with the remaining ingredients until well-coated.
2. Place a crisper plate in both baskets.
3. Add shrimp in both baskets, then insert baskets in the unit.
4. Press zone 1, then select air fry mode.
5. Set the temperature to 392 F/ 200 C and time to 10 minutes.
6. Press MATCH mode, then press start.
7. Serve and enjoy.

CHAPTER 5
POULTRY RECIPES

GARLIC BUTTER CHICKEN WINGS

FLAVORFUL CHICKEN NUGGETS

CHEESY CHICKEN BREAST

CHICKEN CHEESE MEATBALLS

CHICKEN WITH VEGGIES

MUSTARD CHICKEN

JUICY CHICKEN THIGHS

CHICKEN WITH BROCCOLI & POTATOES

MARINATED CHICKEN THIGHS

CURRIED CHICKEN SKEWERS

TASTY CHICKEN BITES

CHICKEN VEGETABLE SKEWERS

LEMON PEPPER CHICKEN WINGS

JUICY & TASTY CHICKEN THIGHS

FLAVORFUL CHICKEN LEGS

GREEK CHICKEN SKEWERS

TURKEY MEATBALLS

ASIAN CHICKEN WINGS

MEATBALLS

SPICY CHICKEN WINGS

Garlic Butter Chicken Wings

Cook time: 25 minutes
Serves: 4
Per Serving: Calories 244, Carbs 0.7g,
Fat 11.3g, Protein 33g

Ingredients:

- Chicken wings - 1 lb
- Pepper - 1/4 tsp
- Garlic powder - 1 tsp
- Salt - 1/2 tsp
  For Sauce:
- Butter, melted - 1 tbsp
- Garlic powder - 1/8 tsp

Directions:

1. Toss chicken wings with pepper, garlic powder, and salt in a mixing bowl.
2. Place a crisper plate in both baskets.
3. Add chicken wings in both baskets, then insert baskets in the unit.
4. Press zone 1, then select air fry mode.
5. Set the temperature to 392 F/ 200 C and time to 25 minutes.
6. Press MATCH mode, then press start.
7. In a large bowl, mix melted butter and garlic powder
8. Add cooked chicken wings and toss until well coated
9. Serve and enjoy.

Flavorful Chicken Nuggets

Cook time: 25 minutes
Serves: 4
Per Serving: Calories 270, Carbs 4g,
Fat 10.4g, Protein 38.1g

Ingredients:

- Chicken breast, chunks - 1 1/2 lbs
- Garlic powder - 1/2 tsp
- Parmesan cheese, shredded - 1/4 cup
- Mayonnaise - 1/4 cup
- Pepper
- Salt

Directions:

1. Mix mayonnaise, cheese, garlic powder, pepper, and salt in a mixing bowl.
2. Add chicken and mix until well-coated.
3. Place a crisper plate in both baskets.
4. Add chicken in both baskets, then insert baskets in the unit.
5. Press zone 1, then select air fry mode.
6. Set the temperature to 392 F/ 200 C and time to 25 minutes.
7. Press MATCH mode, then press start.
8. Serve and enjoy.

Cheesy Chicken Breast

Cook time: 30 minutes
Serves: 4
Per Serving: Calories 505, Carbs 1.9g,
Fat 32g, Protein 50.5g

Ingredients:

- Chicken breasts – 4, boneless & cut a pocket into the side of the chicken breast
- Feta cheese, crumbled - 2 oz
- Cream cheese - 4 oz
- Butter, melted - 2 tbsp
- Dried parsley - 1 tsp
- Mozzarella cheese, shredded - 2 oz
- Pepper
- Salt

Directions:

1. Mix mozzarella cheese, cream cheese, parsley, and feta cheese in a small bowl until well combined.
2. Stuff cheese mixture into each chicken breast and secure the edges with toothpicks.
3. Season chicken with pepper and salt and brush with butter.
4. Place a crisper plate in both baskets.
5. Place stuffed chicken breasts in both baskets, then insert baskets in the unit.
6. Press zone 1, then select bake mode.
7. Set the temperature to 392 F/ 200 C and the time to 30 minutes.
8. Press MATCH mode, then press start.
9. Serve and enjoy.

Chicken Cheese Meatballs

Cook time: 12 minutes
Serves: 4
Per Serving: Calories 550, Carbs 9g,
Fat 27.9g, Protein 62g

Ingredients:

- Eggs, beaten - 2
- Ground chicken - 1 lb
- Onion, diced - 1 cup
- Ham, diced - 1 lb
- Garlic cloves, minced - 4
- Swiss cheese, shredded - 1 cup
- Pepper
- Salt

Directions:

1. Add chicken and remaining ingredients into the mixing bowl until well combined. Place in refrigerator for 40 minutes.
2. Place a crisper plate in both baskets.
3. Remove the chicken mixture from the refrigerator and make equal shapes of meatballs.
4. Place prepared chicken meatballs in both baskets, then insert baskets in the unit.
5. Press zone 1, then select air fry mode.
6. Set the temperature to 392 F/ 200 C and time to 12 minutes.
7. Press MATCH mode, then press start.
8. Serve and enjoy.

Chicken with Veggies

Cook time: 10 minutes
Serves: 4
Per Serving: Calories 226, Carbs 12g,
Fat 7.6g, Protein 26.5g

Ingredients:

- Chicken breast, pieces - 1 lb
- Garlic powder - 1/2 tsp
- Olive oil - 1 tbsp
- Frozen mixed vegetables - 10 oz
- Italian seasoning - 1 tbsp
- Chili powder - 1/2 tsp
- Garlic cloves, minced - 2
- Pepper
- Salt

Directions:

1. In a bowl, toss chicken with chili powder, garlic powder, vegetables, Italian seasoning, oil, garlic, pepper, and salt until well coated.
2. Place a crisper plate in both baskets.
3. Add chicken and vegetable mixture in both baskets, then insert baskets in the unit.
4. Press zone 1, then select air fry mode.
5. Set the temperature to 392 F/ 200 C and the time to 10 minutes.
6. Press MATCH mode, then press start.
7. Serve and enjoy.

Mustard Chicken

Cook time: 12 minutes
Serves: 4
Per Serving: Calories 434, Carbs 18.4g,
Fat 20.7g, Protein 43.1g

Ingredients:

- Chicken breasts, boneless - 4
- Dijon mustard - 1/4 cup
- Honey - 1/4 cup
- Butter, melted - 2 tbsp
- Lemon juice - 2 tsp
- Olive oil - 1 tbsp
- Pepper
- Salt

Directions:

1. Mix butter, mustard, oil, honey, lemon juice, pepper, and salt in a small bowl.
2. Place a crisper plate in both baskets.
3. Brush chicken breasts with butter mixture and place in both baskets, then insert baskets in the unit.
4. Press zone 1, then select air fry mode.
5. Set the temperature to 375 F/ 190 C and the time to 12 minutes.
6. Press MATCH mode, then press start.
7. Serve and enjoy.

Juicy Chicken Thighs

Cook time: 12 minutes
Serves: 8
Per Serving: Calories 230, Carbs 0.7g,
Fat 9.7g, Protein 33g

Ingredients:

- Chicken thighs - 2 lbs
- Ground cumin - 1 tsp
- Chili powder - 2 tsp
- Garlic powder - 1 tsp
- Olive oil - 2 tsp
- Pepper
- Salt

Directions:

1. Mix chicken with oil, garlic powder, chili powder, cumin, pepper, and salt in a mixing bowl until well coated.
2. Place a crisper plate in both baskets.
3. Place chicken in both baskets, then insert baskets in the unit.
4. Press zone 1, then select air fry mode.
5. Set the temperature to 392 F/ 200 C and time to 12 minutes.
6. Press MATCH mode, then press start.
7. Serve and enjoy.

Chicken with Broccoli & Potatoes

Cook time: 25 minutes
Serves: 4
Per Serving: Calories 453, Carbs 50.5g,
Fat 15.8g, Protein 29.3g

Ingredients:

- Chicken breast, cubed - 1 lb
- Potatoes, cubed - 4 medium
- Olive oil - 1/4 cup
- Broccoli florets - 2 cups
- Garlic, minced - 1 tbsp
- Soy sauce - 1 tbsp
- Honey - 3 tbsp
- Pcpper
- Salt

Directions:

1. In a bowl, toss chicken with potatoes, broccoli, oil, honey, soy sauce, garlic, pepper, and salt until well coated.
2. Place a crisper plate in both baskets.
3. Add chicken and vegetable mixture in both baskets, then insert baskets in the unit.
4. Press zone 1, then select air fry mode.
5. Set the temperature to 350 F/ 180 C and time to 25 minutes.
6. Press MATCH mode, then press start.
7. Serve and enjoy.

Marinated Chicken Thighs

Cook time: 14 minutes
Serves: 4
Per Serving: Calories 646, Carbs 22.2g,
Fat 21.7g, Protein 86.9g

Ingredients:
- Chicken thighs, boneless - 8
- Ketchup - 1 tbsp
- Garlic cloves, minced - 4
- Honey - 1/4 cup
- Dried oregano - 1 tsp
- Parsley, chopped - 2 tbsp
- Soy sauce - 1/2 cup

Directions:
1. Add chicken, garlic, honey, oregano, parsley, ketchup, and soy sauce in a mixing bowl until well coated.
2. Cover bowl and place in refrigerator for 8 hours to marinate the chicken.
3. Place a crisper plate in both baskets.
4. Remove chicken from the marinade, place it in both baskets, then insert baskets in the unit.
5. Press zone 1, then select air fry mode.
6. Set the temperature to 392 F/ 200 C and time to 14 minutes.
7. Press MATCH mode, then press start.
8. Serve and enjoy.

Curried Chicken Skewers

Cook time: 15 minutes
Serves: 4
Per Serving: Calories 541, Carbs 16.7g,
Fat 20.7g, Protein 70.2g

Ingredients:
- Chicken thighs, cubed - 2 lbs
- Fresh lime juice - 3 tbsp
- Coconut milk - 1/4 cup
- Thai red curry - 2 tbsp
- Maple syrup - 3 tbsp
- Tamari soy sauce - 1/2 cup

Directions:
1. Add chicken and remaining ingredients into the mixing bowl and mix well.
2. Cover and place in refrigerator for 2-3 hours.
3. Thread marinated chicken onto the soaked skewers.
4. Place a crisper plate in both baskets.
5. Place chicken skewers in both baskets, then insert baskets in the unit.
6. Press zone 1, then select air fry mode.
7. Set the temperature to 350 F/ 180 C and time to 15 minutes.
8. Press MATCH mode, then press start.
9. Serve and enjoy.

Tasty Chicken Bites

Cook time: 20 minutes
Serves: 4
Per Serving: Calories 497, Carbs 0.9g,
Fat 23.9g, Protein 65.8g

Ingredients:
- Chicken thighs, cut into bite-size pieces - 2 lbs
- White pepper - 1/4 tsp
- Onion powder - 1/2 tsp
- Olive oil - 2 tbsp
- Fresh lemon juice - 1/4 cup
- Garlic powder - 1/2 tsp
- Pepper
- Salt

Directions:
1. Add chicken and remaining ingredients into the mixing bowl and mix well. Cover and place in refrigerator for overnight.
2. Place a crisper plate in both baskets.
3. Place marinated chicken in both baskets, then insert baskets in the unit.
4. Press zone 1, then select air fry mode.
5. Set the temperature to 375 F/ 190 C and time to 20 minutes.
6. Press MATCH mode, then press start.
7. Serve and enjoy.

Chicken Vegetable Skewers

Cook time: 15 minutes
Serves: 6
Per Serving: Calories 325, Carbs 8.6g,
Fat 11.5g, Protein 46.8g

Ingredients:
- Chicken breasts, cubed - 2 lbs
- Bell pepper, chopped - 1
- Swerve - 4 tbsp
- Ginger, grated - 1 tsp
- Zucchini, chopped - 2 cups
- Mushrooms, sliced - 8
- Onion, chopped - 1/2
- Garlic cloves, crushed - 6
- Soy sauce - 1/2 cup

Directions:
1. Add chicken and remaining ingredients into the large mixing bowl and mix well. Cover bowl and place in refrigerator overnight.
2. Thread marinated chicken, onion, zucchini, mushrooms, and bell pepper onto the skewers.
3. Place a crisper plate in both baskets.
4. Place chicken skewers in both baskets, then insert baskets in the unit.
5. Press zone 1, then select air fry mode.
6. Set the temperature to 375 F/ 190 C and time to 15 minutes.
7. Press MATCH mode, then press start.
8. Serve and enjoy.

Lemon Pepper Chicken Wings

Cook time: 20 minutes
Serves: 4
Per Serving: Calories 467, Carbs 1.5g,
Fat 20.4g, Protein 65.9g

Ingredients:

- Chicken wings - 2 lbs
- Lemon zest, grated - 2 1/2 tsp
- Garlic salt - 1 tsp
- Olive oil - 1 tbsp
- Black peppercorns, crushed - 2 tsp

Directions:

1. In a bowl, toss chicken wings with peppercorns, oil, lemon zest, and garlic salt until well coated.
2. Place a crisper plate in both baskets.
3. Add chicken wings in both baskets, then insert baskets in the unit.
4. Press zone 1, then select air fry mode.
5. Set the temperature to 350 F/ 180 C and time to 20 minutes.
6. Press MATCH mode, then press start.
7. Serve and enjoy.

Juicy & Tasty Chicken Thighs

Cook time: 20 minutes
Serves: 4
Per Serving: Calories 318, Carbs 9.8g,
Fat 11.2g, Protein 42.8g

Ingredients:

- Chicken thighs, boneless - 4
- Dried oregano - 1 tsp
- Garlic, minced - 1 tsp
- Yellow mustard - 2 tbsp
- Cayenne - 1/4 tsp
- Paprika - 1/2 tsp
- Dried tarragon - 1 tsp
- Honey - 2 tbsp
- Pepper
- Salt

Directions:

1. In a bowl, toss chicken with the remaining ingredients until well coated.
2. Place a crisper plate in both baskets.
3. Add chicken in both baskets, then insert baskets in the unit.
4. Press zone 1, then select air fry mode.
5. Set the temperature to 392 F/ 200 C and the time to 20 minutes.
6. Press MATCH mode, then press start.
7. Serve and enjoy.

Flavorful Chicken Legs

Cook time: 20 minutes
Serves: 6
Per Serving: Calories 321, Carbs 5.5g,
Fat 13.4g, Protein 42.6g

Ingredients:

- Chicken legs - 6
- Garlic powder - 1 tsp
- Onion powder - 1 tsp
- Ground mustard - 1 tsp
- Olive oil - 1 tbsp
- Cayenne - 1/4 tsp
- Smoked paprika - 1 tsp
- Brown sugar - 3 tbsp
- Pepper
- Salt

Directions:

1. Add chicken legs and remaining ingredients into the large bowl and mix well. Cover bowl and place in refrigerator for 2 hours to marinate the chicken.
2. Place a crisper plate in both baskets.
3. Place marinated chicken legs in both baskets, then insert baskets in the unit.
4. Press zone 1, then select air fry mode.
5. Set the temperature to 375 F/ 190 C and time to 20 minutes.
6. Press MATCH mode, then press start.
7. Serve and enjoy.

Greek Chicken Skewers

Cook time: 16 minutes
Serves: 6
Per Serving: Calories 190, Carbs 5.1g,
Fat 12.3g, Protein 15.2g

Ingredients:

- Chicken breasts, boneless & cut into chunks - 2
- Red wine vinegar - 2 tbsp
- Olive oil - 1/4 cup
- Fresh lemon juice - 1
- Garlic cloves, minced - 2
- Grape tomatoes - 1 1/2 cups
- Zucchini, cut into 1-inch pieces - 1
- Onion, cut into pieces - 1
- Oregano - 1 tsp
- Pepper
- Salt

Directions:

1. Add chicken, onion, zucchini, and remaining ingredients into the large bowl and mix well.
2. Cover bowl and place in refrigerator for 2 hours.
3. Thread marinated chicken, onion, zucchini, and tomatoes onto the soaked skewers.
4. Place a crisper plate in both baskets.
5. Place chicken skewers in both baskets, then insert baskets in the unit.
6. Press zone 1, then select air fry mode.
7. Set the temperature to 375 F/ 190 C and time to 16 minutes.
8. Press MATCH mode, then press start.
9. Serve and enjoy.

Turkey Meatballs

Cook time: 10 minutes
Serves: 4
Per Serving: Calories 245, Carbs 1.8g,
Fat 13.7g, Protein 32.9g

Ingredients:

- Egg, lightly beaten - 1
- Ground turkey - 1 lb
- Parsley, minced - 2 tbsp
- Bell pepper, chopped - 1/2
- Mushrooms, diced - 1/2 cup
- Fresh thyme, minced - 1 tsp
- Pepper
- Salt

Directions:

1. Mix turkey, egg, parsley, bell pepper, mushrooms, thyme, pepper, and salt until well combined.
2. Make equal shapes of balls from the turkey mixture.
3. Place a crisper plate in both baskets.
4. Place prepared meatballs in both baskets, then insert baskets in the unit.
5. Press zone 1, then select air fry mode.
6. Set the temperature to 392 F/ 200 C and the time to 10 minutes.
7. Press MATCH mode, then press start.
8. Serve and enjoy.

Asian Chicken Wings

Cook time: 20 minutes
Serves: 4
Per Serving: Calories 501, Carbs 15.1g,
Fat 17g, Protein 67.4g

Ingredients:

- Chicken wings - 2 lbs
- Fresh cilantro, chopped - 1/4 cup
- Fish sauce - 1/4 cup
- Thai sweet chili sauce - 1/3 cup
- Black pepper - 1 tsp
- Ginger, grated - 2 tbsp
- Garlic, minced - 4 tbsp

Directions:

1. Add chicken wings and remaining ingredients into the large bowl and mix until well coated. Cover and place in refrigerator for 1 hour to marinate.
2. Place a crisper plate in both baskets.
3. Place marinated chicken wings in both baskets, then insert baskets in the unit.
4. Press zone 1, then select air fry mode.
5. Set the temperature to 375 F/ 190 C and time t 20 minutes.
6. Press MATCH mode, then press start.
7. Serve and enjoy.

Meatballs

Cook time: 10 minutes
Serves: 4
Per Serving: Calories 359, Carbs 2.6g,
Fat 19.9g, Protein 48.3g

Ingredients:

- Egg, lightly beaten - 1
- Ground turkey - 1 1/2 lbs
- Bell pepper, chopped - 1
- Fresh coriander, minced - 1 tbsp
- Fresh parsley, minced - 1/4 cup
- Paprika - 1/4 tsp
- Pepper
- Salt

Directions:

1. Mix ground turkey, egg, bell pepper, paprika, coriander, parsley, pepper, and salt in a bowl until well combined.
2. Place a crisper plate in both baskets.
3. Make small balls from the meat mixture and place them in both baskets, then insert baskets in the unit.
4. Press zone 1, then select air fry mode.
5. Set the temperature to 350 F/ 180 C and time to 10 minutes.
6. Press MATCH mode, then press start.
7. Serve and enjoy.

Spicy Chicken Wings

Cook time: 30 minutes
Serves: 8
Per Serving: Calories 277, Carbs 2.4g,
Fat 14.4g, Protein 33.2g

Ingredients:

- Chicken wings - 2 lbs
- Brown sugar - 1 tbsp
- Chili powder - 1 tbsp
- Butter, melted - 1/4 cup
- Smoked paprika - 1 tsp
- Garlic powder - 1 tsp
- Black pepper - 1 tsp
- Salt - 1 tsp

Directions:

1. In a mixing bowl, toss chicken wings with chili powder, garlic powder, smoked paprika, butter, brown sugar, black pepper, and salt until well coated.
2. Place a crisper plate in both baskets.
3. Add chicken wings in both baskets, then insert baskets in the unit.
4. Press zone 1, then select air fry mode.
5. Set the temperature to 392 F/ 200 C and the time to 30 minutes.
6. Press MATCH mode, then press start.
7. Serve and enjoy.

CHAPTER 6
MEAT RECIPES

Meatballs

Cook time: 20 minutes
Serves: 6
Per Serving: Calories 294, Carbs 0.9g,
Fat 10.2g, Protein 46.9g

Ingredients:

- Ground beef - 2 lbs
- Egg, lightly beaten - 1
- Oregano - 1 tsp
- Cinnamon - 1 tsp
- Garlic, minced - 1 tsp
- Allspice - 1/2 tsp
- Pepper - 1/4 tsp
- Salt - 1/2 tsp

Directions:

1. Add ground meat and remaining ingredients into the mixing bowl and mix until well combined.
2. Place a crisper plate in both baskets.
3. Make small balls from the meat mixture and place them in both baskets, then insert baskets in the unit.
4. Press zone 1, then select bake mode.
5. Set the temperature to 392 F/ 200 C and time to 20 minutes.
6. Press MATCH mode, then press start.
7. Serve and enjoy.

Garlic Butter Sirloin Steak

Cook time: 40 minutes
Serves: 6
Per Serving: Calories 365, Carbs 2g,
Fat 18g, Protein 45g

Ingredients:

- Sirloin steak cut into 1-inch cubes - 2 lbs
- Water - 1/4 cup
- Butter, melted - 1/4 cup
- Garlic cloves, minced - 2
- Dried oregano - 1 tsp
- Pepper - 1/2 tsp
- Salt - 1 tsp

Directions:

1. Add meat and remaining ingredients into the mixing bowl and mix well. Cover bowl and place in refrigerator for 1 hour.
2. Place a crisper plate in both baskets.
3. Place marinated beef in both baskets, then insert baskets in the unit.
4. Press zone 1, then select bake mode.
5. Set the temperature to 392 F/ 200 C and time to 30 minutes.
6. Press MATCH mode, then press start.
7. Serve and enjoy.

Marinated Lamb Chops

Cook time: 30 minutes
Serves: 8
Per Serving: Calories 651, Carbs 10.5g,
Fat 24.1g, Protein 92.1g

Ingredients:

- Lamb chops - 8
- Tarragon - 3 tsp
- Ginger - 3 tsp
- Brown sugar - 1/2 cup
- Garlic powder - 2 tsp
- Ground cinnamon - 2 tsp
- Pepper
- Salt

Directions:

1. Add lamb chops and remaining ingredients into the large mixing bowl and mix until well coated. Cover the bowl and place in the refrigerator for 2 hours.
2. Place a crisper plate in both baskets.
3. Place marinated lamb chops in both baskets, then insert baskets in the unit.
4. Press zone 1, then select bake mode.
5. Set the temperature to 375 F/ 190 C and time to 30 minutes.
6. Press MATCH mode, then press start.
7. Serve and enjoy.

Easy Pork Patties

Cook time: 35 minutes
Serves: 6
Per Serving: Calories 255, Carbs 3.8g,
Fat 7.3g, Protein 41.4g

Ingredients:

- Egg - 1
- Ground pork - 2 lbs
- Carrot, minced - 1
- Garlic powder - 1 tsp
- Smoked paprika - 1 tsp
- Almond flour - 1/2 cup
- Onion, minced - 1
- Pepper
- Salt

Directions:

1. Add ground meat and remaining ingredients into the bowl and mix until well combined.
2. Make equal shapes of patties from the meat mixture.
3. Place a crisper plate in both baskets.
4. Place prepared patties in both baskets, then insert baskets in the unit.
5. Press zone 1, then select air fry mode.
6. Set the temperature to 375 F/ 190 C and time to 35 minutes.
7. Press MATCH mode, then press start.
8. Serve and enjoy.

Simple Beef Kababs

Cook time: 15 minutes
Serves: 8
Per Serving: Calories 178, Carbs 3.9g,
Fat 5.5g, Protein 26.9g

Ingredients:

- Beef, cut into 1-inch pieces - 1 1/2 lbs
- Bell peppers, cut into chunks - 2
- Greek yogurt - 1/4 cup
- Garlic, minced - 1 tsp
- Onion, cut into chunks - 1
- Paprika - 1/4 tsp
- Pepper
- Salt

Directions:

1. Add meat and remaining ingredients into the mixing bowl and mix well. Cover and place in refrigerator for 20 minutes.
2. Thread marinated meat, onion, and bell pepper pieces onto the soaked wooden skewers.
3. Place a crisper plate in both baskets.
4. Place meat skewers in both baskets, then insert baskets in the unit.
5. Press zone 1, then select air fry mode.
6. Set the temperature to 350 F/ 180 C and the time to 15 minutes.
7. Press MATCH mode, then press start.
8. Serve and enjoy.

Steak Skewers

Cook time: 8 minutes
Serves: 4
Per Serving: Calories 462, Carbs 5.7g,
Fat 24.5g, Protein 52.4g

Ingredients:

- Sirloin steak cut into 1-inch chunks - 1 1/2 lbs
- Chili powder - 1/2 tsp
- Canola oil - 1/4 cup
- Lemon juice - 1 tbsp
- Onion, cut into pieces - 1
- Bell pepper, cut into pieces - 1
- Cumin - 1/2 tsp
- Garlic cloves, minced - 3
- Pepper
- Salt

Directions:

1. Add steak pieces and remaining ingredients into the mixing bowl and mix well. Cover and place in refrigerator for 12 hours to marinate.
2. Thread marinated steak pieces onto the soaked skewers.
3. Place a crisper plate in both baskets.
4. Place meat skewers in both baskets, then insert baskets in the unit.
5. Press zone 1, then select air fry mode.
6. Set the temperature to 392 F/ 200 C and time to 8 minutes.
7. Press MATCH mode, then press start.
8. Serve and enjoy.

Meatballs

Cook time: 10 minutes
Serves: 12
Per Serving: Calories 141, Carbs 3.6g,
Fat 4g, Protein 21.4g

Ingredients:

- Eggs - 2
- Ground pork - 2 lbs
- Sesame oil - 1 tsp
- Ginger, minced - 1 tsp
- Garlic, minced - 1 tsp
- Breadcrumbs - 1/2 cup
- Red pepper flakes - 1/3 tsp
- Scallions, chopped - 1 tbsp
- Soy sauce - 1 tsp
- Pepper
- Salt

Directions:

1. Add ground pork and remaining ingredients into the bowl and mix until well combined.
2. Place a crisper plate in both baskets.
3. Make small balls from the meat mixture and place them in both baskets, then insert baskets in the unit.
4. Press zone 1, then select air fry mode.
5. Set the temperature to 392 F/ 200 C and time to 10 minutes.
6. Press MATCH mode, then press start.
7. Serve and enjoy.

Flavorful Herb Lamb Chops

Cook time: 6 minutes
Serves: 8
Per Serving: Calories 217, Carbs 1g,
Fat 12.7g, Protein 24g

Ingredients:

- Lamb chops - 8
- Olive oil - 1/4 cup
- Thyme, chopped - 1 tbsp
- Garlic cloves, minced - 2
- Lemon zest - 1
- Rosemary, chopped - 1 tbsp
- Dried oregano - 1/2 tsp
- Lemon juice - 2 tbsp
- Pepper
- Salt

Directions:

1. Add lamb chops and remaining ingredients into the large mixing bowl and mix well. Cover and place in refrigerator for 30 minutes.
2. Place a crisper plate in both baskets.
3. Place marinated lamb chops in both baskets, then insert baskets in the unit.
4. Press zone 1, then select air fry mode.
5. Set the temperature to 392 F/ 200 C and time to 6 minutes.
6. Press MATCH mode, then press start.
7. Serve and enjoy.

Juicy Lamb Chops

Cook time: 6 minutes
Serves: 8
Per Serving: Calories 350, Carbs 9.2g,
Fat 12.5g, Protein 47.9g

Ingredients:

- Lamb chops - 16
- Garlic powder - 1 tsp
- Cayenne - 1/2 tsp
- Honey - 1/4 cup
- Onion powder - 1/2 tsp
- Pepper
- Salt

Directions:

1. Add lamb chops and remaining ingredients into the mixing bowl and mix well. Cover and set aside for 15 minutes.
2. Place a crisper plate in both baskets.
3. Place lamb chops in both baskets, then insert baskets in the unit.
4. Press zone 1, then select air fry mode.
5. Set the temperature to 392 F/ 200 C and time to 6 minutes.
6. Press MATCH mode, then press start.
7. Serve and enjoy.

Garlic Mint Lamb Chops

Cook time: 15 minutes
Serves: 4
Per Serving: Calories 711, Carbs 5.5g,
Fat 44g, Protein 72.3g

Ingredients:

- Lamb loin chops - 12
- Fresh mint, chopped - 1/4 cup
- Lime zest - 1 tbsp
- Olive oil - 1/2 cup
- Lime juice - 3
- Garlic cloves, minced - 8
- Pepper
- Salt

Directions:

1. Add lamb chops and remaining ingredients into the large mixing bowl and mix well. Cover and place in refrigerator for 4 hours.
2. Place a crisper plate in both baskets.
3. Remove lamb chops from the marinade, place them in both baskets, then insert baskets in the unit.
4. Press zone 1, then select air fry mode.
5. Set the temperature to 350 F/ 180 C and time to 15 minutes.
6. Press MATCH mode, then press start.
7. Serve and enjoy.

Parmesan Pork Chops

Cook time: 12 minutes
Serves: 6
Per Serving: Calories 386, Carbs 1g,
Fat 29.8g, Protein 27.2g

Ingredients:

- Pork chops, boneless - 1 1/2 lbs
- Parmesan cheese, grated - 1/4 cup
- Almond flour - 1/3 cup
- Paprika - 1 tsp
- Creole seasoning - 1 tsp
- Garlic powder - 1 tsp

Directions:

1. Add pork chops and remaining ingredients into the large mixing bowl and mix until well coated.
2. Place a crisper plate in both baskets.
3. Place coated pork chops in both baskets, then insert baskets in the unit.
4. Press zone 1, then select air fry mode.
5. Set the temperature to 350 F/ 180 C and the time to 12 minutes.
6. Press MATCH mode, then press start.
7. Serve and enjoy.

Marinated Steak Kababs

Cook time: 8 minutes
Serves: 8
Per Serving: Calories 246, Carbs 13.3g,
Fat 11g, Protein 22.4g

Ingredients:

- Steak, cut into 1-inch cubes - 1 lb
- Olive oil - 1/4 cup
- Worcestershire sauce - 1/2 cup
- Soy sauce - 1/2 cup
- Mixed vegetables - 2 cups
- Sriracha - 1 tsp
- Sesame oil - 1 tbsp
- Spicy mustard - 2 tbsp
- Brown sugar - 1/4 cup

Directions:

1. Add steak, mixed vegetables, and remaining ingredients into the mixing bowl and mix well. Cover and place in refrigerator for 2 hours.
2. Thread marinated steak pieces and vegetables onto the soaked skewers.
3. Place a crisper plate in both baskets.
4. Place skewers in both baskets, then insert baskets in the unit.
5. Press zone 1, then select air fry mode.
6. Set the temperature to 350 F/ 180 C and the time to 8 minutes.
7. Press MATCH mode, then press start.
8. Serve and enjoy.

Sausage Balls

Cook time: 6 minutes
Serves: 6
Per Serving: Calories 630, Carbs 26g,
Fat 46.7g, Protein 25.4g

Ingredients:

- Pork sausage - 1 lb
- Cheddar cheese, shredded - 1 cup
- Bisquick - 2 cups
- Cream cheese - 8 oz
- Onion powder - 1 tsp
- Garlic powder - 1 tsp
- Pepper
- Salt

Directions:

1. Add pork sausage and remaining ingredients into the mixing bowl and mix until well combined.
2. Place a crisper plate in both baskets.
3. Make small balls from the sausage mixture and place them in both baskets, then insert baskets in the unit.
4. Press zone 1, then select air fry mode.
5. Set the temperature to 392 F/ 200 C and time to 6 minutes.
6. Press MATCH mode, then press start.
7. Serve and enjoy.

Sausage with Broccoli & Sweet Potatoes

Cook time: 15 minutes
Serves: 4
Per Serving: Calories 470, Carbs 23.9g,
Fat 31.9g, Protein 21.7g

Ingredients:

- Smoked sausage, sliced - 14 oz
- Cajun seasoning - 2 tsp
- Sweet potatoes, peeled & cubed - 2
- Olive oil - 1 tbsp
- Broccoli florets - 2 cups

Directions:

1. Place a crisper plate in both baskets.
2. Toss sweet potatoes with oil in a bowl and add them to the first basket.
3. Press zone 1, then select air fry mode.
4. Set the temperature to 392 F/ 200 C and time to 10 minutes.
5. In a bowl, toss broccoli, sausage, and Cajun seasoning.
6. Add broccoli and sausage mixture into the second basket.
7. Press zone 2, then select air fry mode.
8. Set the temperature to 392 F/ 200 C and time to 5 minutes. Press start.
9. Add sweet potatoes to the broccoli sausage mixture and mix well.
10. Serve and enjoy.

Beef Burger Patties

Cook time: 15 minutes
Serves: 8
Per Serving: Calories 309, Carbs 4.7g,
Fat 14g, Protein 38.7g

Ingredients:

- Ground beef - 2 lbs
- Onion, chopped - 1 cup
- Olives, pitted & chopped - 1/2 cup
- Feta cheese, crumbled - 1 cup
- Garlic powder - 1/2 tsp
- Montreal steak seasoning - 1 tsp
- Worcestershire sauce - 4 tbsp
- Salt

Directions:

1. Add ground beef and remaining ingredients into the mixing bowl and mix until well combined.
2. Make eight equal shapes of patties from the meat mixture.
3. Place a crisper plate in both baskets.
4. Place patties in both baskets, then insert baskets in the unit.
5. Press zone 1, then select air fry mode.
6. Set the temperature to 392 F/ 200 C and time to 15 minutes.
7. Press MATCH mode, then press start.
8. Serve and enjoy.

Sweet and savory Pork Chops

Cook time: 25 minutes
Serves: 4
Per Serving: Calories 839, Carbs 11.2g,
Fat 64.3g, Protein 51.9g

Ingredients:

- Pork chops, bone-in - 2 lbs
- Onion powder - 2 tsp
- Ground mustard - 1 tbsp
- Paprika - 1 tsp
- Olive oil - 2 tbsp
- Brown sugar - 1/4 cup
- Pepper
- Salt

Directions:

1. Mix paprika, onion powder, brown sugar, pepper, ground mustard, and salt in a small bowl.
2. Brush pork chops with oil and rub with spice mixture.
3. Place a crisper plate in both baskets.
4. Place pork chops in both baskets, then insert baskets in the unit.
5. Press zone 1, then select air fry mode.
6. Set the temperature to 375 F/ 190 C and time to 25 minutes.
7. Press MATCH mode, then press start.
8. Serve and enjoy.

Marinated Spare Ribs

Cook time: 20 minutes
Serves: 6
Per Serving: Calories 388, Carbs 22.9g,
Fat 18.1g, Protein 31.5g

Ingredients:

- Country-style pork ribs, sliced into 1-inch pieces - 2 lbs
- Honey - 2 tbsp
- Brown sugar - 4 tbsp
- Soy sauce - 1/4 cup
- Hoisin sauce - 1/2 cup
- Ginger, minced - 1 tsp
- Garlic powder - 1 tsp
- Five-spice powder - 1 tbsp

Directions:

1. Add pork ribs and remaining ingredients into the large bowl and mix well. Cover and place in refrigerator for 2 hours.
2. Place a crisper plate in both baskets.
3. Remove pork ribs from the marinade, place them in both baskets, then insert baskets in the unit.
4. Press zone 1, then select air fry mode.
5. Set the temperature to 392 F/ 200 C and time to 20 minutes.
6. Press MATCH mode, then press start.
7. Serve and enjoy.

Sausage with Baby Potatoes

Cook time: 20 minutes
Serves: 4
Per Serving: Calories 554, Carbs 23.3g,
Fat 39.4g, Protein 26.7g

Ingredients:

- Smoked sausage, sliced - 16 oz
- Small onion, sliced - 1
- Baby potatoes, cut in half - 1 1/2 lbs
- Dried parsley - 1 tsp
- Garlic powder - 1 tsp
- Canola oil - 2 tbsp
- Pepper
- Salt

Directions:

1. Place a crisper plate in both baskets.
2. Toss potatoes with onion, parsley, pepper, oil, garlic powder, and salt in a bowl.
3. Add potatoes to the first basket.
4. Press zone 1, then select air fry mode.
5. Set the temperature to 392 F/ 200 C and time to 15 minutes.
6. Add sausage slices into the second basket.
7. Press zone 2, then select air fry mode.
8. Set the temperature to 392 F/ 200 C and time to 5 minutes. Press start.
9. Add sausage slices to the potato mixture and mix well.
10. Serve and enjoy.

Steak with Mushrooms

Cook time: 20 minutes
Serves: 4
Per Serving: Calories 300, Carbs 2.4g,
Fat 12.8g, Protein 42.8g

Ingredients:

- Steaks, cut into 1-inch pieces - 1 lb
- Olive oil - 2 tbsp
- Mushrooms, cleaned & halved - 8 oz
- Garlic powder - 1/2 tsp
- Worcestershire sauce - 1 tsp
- Pepper
- Salt

Directions:

1. Mix steak pieces, olive oil, mushrooms, garlic powder, Worcestershire sauce, pepper, and salt in a bowl.
2. Place a crisper plate in both baskets.
3. Add steak and mushroom mixture in both baskets, then insert baskets in the unit.
4. Press zone 1, then select air fry mode.
5. Set the temperature to 392 F/ 200 C and the tim to 20 minutes.
6. Press MATCH mode, then press start.
7. Serve and enjoy.

Garlic Herb Sirloin Steak

Cook time: 10 minutes
Serves: 4
Per Serving: Calories 229, Carbs 2.2g,
Fat 120.4g, Protein 25.9g

Ingredients:

- Sirloin steaks - 4
- Thyme chopped - 1 tbsp
- Olive oil - 2 tbsp
- Steak sauce - 2 tbsp
- Ground coriander - 1/2 tsp
- Garlic, minced - 1 tsp
- Pepper
- Salt

Directions:

1. Mix steak with oil, sauce, coriander, garlic, thyme, pepper, and salt in a large bowl. Cover and set aside for 30 minutes.
2. Place a crisper plate in both baskets.
3. Place marinated steak in both baskets, then insert baskets in the unit.
4. Press zone 1, then select air fry mode.
5. Set the temperature to 350 F/ 180 C and time to 10 minutes.
6. Press MATCH mode, then press start.
7. Serve and enjoy.

CHAPTER 7
VEGETABLE RECIPES

HEALTHY STUFFED PEPPERS

BAKED CARROT FRIES

CINNAMON HONEY BUTTERNUT SQUASH

BROCCOLI SQUASH & PEPPER

BALSAMIC MIXED VEGETABLES

MEXICAN CAULIFLOWER FLORETS

MUSHROOMS ZUCCHINI PEPPER

PARMESAN EGGPLANT SLICES

ROASTED CARROTS & POTATOES

HEALTHY GREEK VEGETABLES

Healthy Stuffed Peppers

Cook time: 25 minutes
Serves: 6
Per Serving: Calories 237, Carbs 39.8g,
Fat 4.8g, Protein 9.8g

Ingredients:
- Bell peppers, cut in half & remove seeds - 3
- Cooked quinoa - 1 1/2 cups
- Chickpeas, rinsed - 1/3 cup
- Oregano - 1/2 tsp
- Feta cheese, crumbled - 1/4 cup
- Cherry tomatoes, sliced - 1/2 cup
- Garlic cloves, minced - 2
- Salt - 1/2 tsp

Directions:
1. Mix quinoa, oregano, garlic, tomatoes, chickpeas, and salt in a bowl.
2. Stuff the quinoa mixture into the bell pepper halves.
3. Place a crisper plate in both baskets.
4. Place stuffed peppers in both baskets, then insert baskets in the unit.
5. Press zone 1, then select bake mode.
6. Set the temperature to 392 F/ 200 C and time to 25 minutes.
7. Press MATCH mode, then press start.
8. Serve and enjoy.

Baked Carrot Fries

Cook time: 20 minutes
Serves: 6
Per Serving: Calories 104, Carbs 15.4g,
Fat 4.8g, Protein 1.3g

Ingredients:
- Carrots peeled & cut into fries' shape - 2 lbs
- Olive oil - 2 tbsp
  Spice mixture:
- Chili flakes - 1/4 tsp
- Dried oregano - 2 tsp
- Dried basil - 2 tsp
- Dried rosemary - 1 tsp
- Dried parsley - 3 tsp
- Salt - 1 tsp

Directions:
1. Add all spice ingredients into the mixing bowl and mix well.
2. Add carrots and oil and toss well to coat.
3. Place a crisper plate in both baskets.
4. Add carrot fries in both baskets, then insert baskets in the unit.
5. Press zone 1, then select bake mode.
6. Set the temperature to 392 F/ 200 C and time to 20 minutes.
7. Press MATCH mode, then press start.
8. Serve and enjoy.

Cinnamon Honey Butternut Squash

Cook time: 40 minutes
Serves: 4
Per Serving: Calories 220, Carbs 45.1g,
Fat 5.6g, Protein 3.4g

Ingredients:

- Butternut squash, peeled, seeded, and cut into 1-inch cubes - 3 lbs
- Cinnamon - 1/2 tsp
- Olive oil - 1 1/2 tbsp
- Honey - 1 1/2 tbsp
- Pepper - to taste
- Salt - to taste

Directions:

In a bowl, toss squash cubes with the remaining ingredients.

Place a crisper plate in both baskets.

Spread squash cubes in both baskets, then insert baskets in the unit.

4. Press zone 1, then select bake mode.
5. Set the temperature to 392 F/ 200 C and time to 40 minutes.
6. Press MATCH mode, then press start.
7. Serve and enjoy.

Broccoli Squash & Pepper

Cook time: 12 minutes
Serves: 4
Per Serving: Calories 75, Carbs 9.6g,
Fat 3.9g, Protein 2.9g

Ingredients:

- Broccoli florets - 1 cup
- Yellow squash, sliced - 2
- Red bell pepper, diced - 1
- Olive oil - 1 tbsp
- Onion, sliced - 1/4
- Zucchini, sliced - 1
- Garlic powder - 1/2 tsp
- Pepper
- Salt

Directions:

Toss vegetables with oil, pepper, garlic powder, and salt in a bowl.

Place a crisper plate in both baskets.

Add veggie mixture in both baskets, then insert baskets in the unit.

4. Press zone 1, then select air fry mode.
5. Set the temperature to 392 F/ 200 C and time to 12 minutes.
6. Press MATCH mode, then press start.
7. Serve and enjoy.

Balsamic Mixed Vegetables

Cook time: 13 minutes
Serves: 4
Per Serving: Calories 184, Carbs 14.7g,
Fat 13.3g, Protein 5.5g

Ingredients:

- Asparagus cut woody ends off - 8 oz
- Cherry tomatoes - 6 oz
- Olive oil - 1/4 cup
- Mushrooms, halved - 8 oz
- Zucchini, sliced - 1
- Yellow squash, sliced - 1
- Dijon mustard - 1 tbsp
- Soy sauce - 3 tbsp
- Brown sugar - 2 tbsp
- Balsamic vinegar - 1/4 cup
- Pepper
- Salt

Directions:

1. Mix asparagus, squash, tomatoes, oil, mushrooms, zucchini, mustard, soy sauce, brown sugar, vinegar, pepper, and salt in a mixing bowl.
2. Cover bowl and place in refrigerator for 40 minutes.
3. Place a crisper plate in both baskets.
4. Add veggie mixture in both baskets, then insert baskets in the unit.
5. Press zone 1, then select air fry mode.
6. Set the temperature to 392 F/ 200 C and time t 13 minutes.
7. Press MATCH mode, then press start.
8. Serve and enjoy.

Mexican Cauliflower Florets

Cook time: 10 minutes
Serves: 4
Per Serving: Calories 111, Carbs 10.9g,
Fat 7.4g, Protein 3.4g

Ingredients:

- Medium cauliflower head cut into florets - 1
- Turmeric - 1/2 tsp
- Onion powder - 1 tsp
- Garlic powder - 2 tsp
- Lime juice - 1 lime
- Olive oil - 2 tbsp
- Chili powder - 1 tsp
- Parsley - 2 tsp
- Cumin - 1 tsp
- Pepper
- Salt

Directions:

1. In a bowl, toss cauliflower florets with onion powder, garlic powder, oil, chili powder, turmeric, parsley, cumin, pepper, and salt.
2. Place a crisper plate in both baskets.
3. Add cauliflower florets in both baskets, then insert baskets in the unit.
4. Press zone 1, then select air fry mode.
5. Set the temperature to 392 F/ 200 C and time to 12 minutes.
6. Press MATCH mode, then press start.
7. Serve and enjoy.

Mushrooms Zucchini Pepper

Cook time: 12 minutes
Serves: 4
Per Serving: Calories 58, Carbs 6g,
Fat 3.7g, Protein 2.4g

Ingredients:

- Small zucchini, sliced - 1
- Olive oil - 1 tbsp
- Red bell pepper cut into pieces - 1
- Mushrooms, quartered - 6
- Small onion, sliced - 1
- Garlic powder - 1/2 tsp
- Pepper
- Salt

Directions:

1. Toss mushrooms, bell pepper, garlic powder, onion, zucchini, oil, pepper, and salt in a bowl.
2. Place a crisper plate in both baskets.
3. Add vegetable mixture in both baskets, then insert baskets in the unit.
4. Press zone 1, then select air fry mode.
5. Set the temperature to 392 F/ 200 C and time to 12 minutes.
6. Press MATCH mode, then press start.
7. Serve and enjoy.
8.

Parmesan Eggplant Slices

Cook time: 12 minutes
Serves: 8
Per Serving: Calories 156, Carbs 3.7g,
Fat 15.8g, Protein 1.5g

Ingredients:

- Medium eggplant, cut into 1-inch-thick slices - 1
- Parmesan cheese, grated - 1 tbsp
- Butter, melted - 4 oz
- Italian seasoning - 1 tsp
- Garlic, minced - 1 tsp
- Olive oil - 2 tbsp
- Pepper
- Salt

Directions:

1. Brush eggplant slices with oil and season with Italian seasoning, pepper, and salt.
2. Place a crisper plate in both baskets.
3. Place eggplant slices in both baskets, then insert baskets in the unit.
4. Press zone 1, then select air fry mode.
5. Set the temperature to 392 F/ 200 C and time to 12 minutes.
6. Press MATCH mode, then press start.
7. In a small bowl, mix butter, garlic, and parmesan cheese.
8. Brush cooked eggplant slices with butter mixture.
9. Serve and enjoy.

Roasted Carrots & Potatoes

Cook time: 25 minutes
Serves: 8
Per Serving: Calories 101, Carbs 16.6g,
Fat 3.6g, Protein 1.6g

Ingredients:

- Potatoes, diced - 1 lb
- Carrots, sliced - 1 lb
- Garlic powder - 1 tsp
- Smoked paprika - 2 tsp
- Sugar - 1 tbsp
- Thyme - 1/4 tsp
- Dried oregano - 1/2 tsp
- Olive oil - 2 tbsp
- Pepper
- Salt

Directions:

1. In a bowl, toss carrots and potatoes with 1 tablespoon of oil.
2. Place a crisper plate in both baskets.
3. Add carrots and potatoes in both baskets, then insert baskets in the unit.
4. Press zone 1, then select air fry mode.
5. Set the temperature to 392 F/ 200 C and time to 15 minutes.
6. Press MATCH mode, then press start.
7. Add cooked carrots, potatoes, remaining oil, sugar, pepper, thyme, oregano, garlic powder, smoked paprika, and salt in a mixing bowl and toss well.
8. Return the carrot and potato mixture to the air fryer basket and cook for 10 minutes more.
9. Serve and enjoy.

Healthy Greek Vegetables

Cook time: 15 minutes
Serves: 6
Per Serving: Calories 140, Carbs 22g,
Fat 5.6g, Protein 4.9g

Ingredients:

- Mushrooms, sliced - 1 cup
- Olive oil - 2 tbsp
- Yellow squash, cut into cubes - 1
- Zucchini, cut into cubes - 1
- Eggplants, cut into cubes - 2
- Cherry tomatoes - 12
- Onion, diced - 1/2
- Balsamic vinegar - 2 tbsp
- Pepper
- Salt

Directions:

1. Toss vegetables with oil, pepper, vinegar, and salt in a bowl.
2. Place a crisper plate in both baskets.
3. Add vegetable mixture in both baskets, then insert baskets in the unit.
4. Press zone 1, then select air fry mode.
5. Set the temperature to 392 F/ 200 C and time to 15 minutes.
6. Press MATCH mode, then press start.
7. Serve and enjoy.

CHAPTER 8
DESSERTS

BLUEBERRY MUFFINS

DELICIOUS CARROT MUFFINS

SWEET CINNAMON FIGS

SOFT & FLUFFY DONUTS

LEMON CHEESE MUFFINS

CINNAMON PINEAPPLE SLICES

QUICK PEANUT BUTTER COOKIES

CHOCOLATE BROWNIE MUFFINS

EASY SEMOLINA PUDDING

TASTY APPLE FRITTERS

Blueberry Muffins

Cook time: 14 minutes
Serves: 8
Per Serving: Calories 221, Carbs 30g,
Fat 9g, Protein 2.9g

Ingredients:

- Egg - 1
- All-purpose flour - 1 1/3 cups
- Vegetable oil - 1/3 cup
- Baking powder - 2 tsp
- Fresh blueberries - 2/3 cup
- Sugar - ½ cup
- Pinch of salt

Directions:

1. Mix flour, baking powder, sugar, and salt in a mixing bowl.
2. Whisk together egg, oil, and milk in a separate bowl until well combined.
3. Pour the egg mixture into the flour mixture and mix until well combined. Add blueberries and fold well.
4. Spoon batter into the silicone muffin molds.
5. Place a crisper plate in both baskets.
6. Place muffin molds in both baskets, then inser baskets in the unit.
7. Press zone 1, then select bake mode.
8. Set the temperature to 320 F/ 160 C and time t 14 minutes.
9. Press MATCH mode, then press start.
10. Serve and enjoy.

Delicious Carrot Muffins

Cook time: 20 minutes
Serves: 8
Per Serving: Calories 260, Carbs 30g,
Fat 15g, Protein 3.7g

Ingredients:

- Carrot, shredded - 1 1/2 cups
- All-purpose flour - 1 cup
- Butter, melted - 1/2 cup
- Baking soda - 1/2 tsp
- Baking powder - 1 tsp
- Unsweetened almond milk - 1/2 cup
- Brown sugar - 1/3 cup
- Sugar - 1/3 cup
- Walnuts, chopped - 1/3 cup
- Cinnamon - ¾ tsp
- Salt - 1/4 tsp

Directions:

1. In a bowl, whisk melted butter and milk.
2. Add remaining ingredients except for walnuts and carrot and mix until well combined.
3. Add carrots and walnuts and mix well.
4. Spoon the batter into the silicone muffin molds.
5. Place a crisper plate in both baskets.
6. Place muffin molds in both baskets, then inse baskets in the unit.
7. Press zone 1, then select air fry mode.
8. Set the temperature to 320 F/ 160 C and time t 20 minutes.
9. Press MATCH mode, then press start.
10. Serve and enjoy.

Sweet Cinnamon Figs

Cook time: 10 minutes
Serves: 4
Per Serving: Calories 294, Carbs 75g,
Fat 0.9g, Protein 3.3g

Ingredients:

- Fresh figs, cut in half lengthwise - 2 cups
- Cinnamon - 1 tsp
- Sugar - 1/4 cup

Directions:

1. In a small bowl, mix cinnamon and sugar.
2. Coat each fig cut side with a cinnamon sugar mixture.
3. Place a crisper plate in both baskets.
4. Place figs in both baskets, then insert baskets in the unit.
5. Press zone 1, then select air fry mode.
6. Set the temperature to 392 F/ 200 C and time to 10 minutes.
7. Press MATCH mode, then press start.
8. Serve and enjoy.

Soft & Fluffy Donuts

Cook time: 15 minutes
Serves: 12
Per Serving: Calories 143, Carbs 21g,
Fat 5g, Protein 2g

Ingredients:

- Eggs - 2
- All-purpose flour - 1 cup
- Vegetable oil - 1/4 cup
- Sugar - 3/4 cup
- Vanilla - 1/2 tsp
- Baking powder - 1 tsp
- Buttermilk - 1/2 cup
- Salt - 1/2 tsp

Directions:

1. Mix oil, sugar, eggs, vanilla, baking powder, buttermilk, and salt until well combined.
2. Add flour and mix until well combined.
3. Pour batter into the silicone donut molds.
4. Place a crisper plate in both baskets.
5. Place donut molds in both baskets, then insert baskets in the unit.
6. Press zone 1, then select bake mode.
7. Set the temperature to 350 F/ 180 C and time to 15 minutes.
8. Press MATCH mode, then press start.
9. Serve and enjoy.

Lemon Cheese Muffins

Cook time: 20 minutes
Serves: 12
Per Serving: Calories 240, Carbs 33g,
Fat 9g, Protein 5g

Ingredients:

- Egg - 1
- Baking powder - 1/2 tsp
- All-purpose flour - 2 cups
- Lemon zest, grated - 1 tbsp
- Butter softened - 1/2 cup
- Ricotta cheese - 1 cup
- Lemon extract - 1 tsp
- Sugar - 1 cup
- Lemon juice - 1 tbsp
- Baking soda - 1/2 tsp
- Salt - 1/2 tsp

Directions:

1. In a bowl, beat egg, sugar, and butter. Add lemon zest, extract, juice, and ricotta cheese and mix well.
2. Mix flour, baking powder, baking soda, and salt in a separate bowl.
3. Add flour mixture into the egg mixture and mix until well combined.
4. Spoon batter into the silicone muffin molds.
5. Place a crisper plate in both baskets.
6. Place muffin molds in both baskets, then insert baskets in the unit.
7. Press zone 1, then select bake mode.
8. Set the temperature to 350 F/ 180 C and time to 20 minutes.
9. Press MATCH mode, then press start.
10. Serve and enjoy.

Cinnamon Pineapple Slices

Cook time: 10 minutes
Serves: 4
Per Serving: Calories 70, Carbs 18g,
Fat 0g, Protein 0g

Ingredients:

- Pineapple, cut into slices - 1/2
- Honey - 2 tsp
- Ground cinnamon - 1/2 tsp

Directions:

1. In a small bowl, mix cinnamon and honey.
2. Brush pineapple slices with cinnamon honey mixture.
3. Place a crisper plate in both baskets.
4. Place pineapple slices in both baskets, then insert baskets in the unit.
5. Press zone 1, then select air fry mode.
6. Set the temperature to 350 F/ 180 C and time to 10 minutes.
7. Press MATCH mode, then press start.
8. Serve and enjoy.

Quick Peanut Butter Cookies

Cook time: 7 minutes
Serves: 8
Per Serving: Calories 385, Carbs 44g,
Fat 20g, Protein 7g

Ingredients:

- Egg - 1
- All-purpose flour - 1 3/4 cups
- Peanut butter, smooth - 1/2 cup
- Butter, softened - 1/2 cup
- Baking soda - 3/4 tsp
- Milk - 2 tbsp
- Sugar - 1/2 cup
- Brown sugar - 1/2 cup
- Salt - 1/2 tsp

Directions:

1. In a bowl, beat peanut butter and butter using a hand mixer until smooth.
2. Add brown sugar, sugar, milk, and egg, and beat well.
3. Add flour, baking soda, and salt and mix until combined.
4. Place a crisper plate in both baskets.
5. Line both baskets with parchment paper.
6. Make cookies from the mixture and place them in both baskets, then insert baskets in the unit.
7. Press zone 1, then select air fry mode.
8. Set the temperature to 350 F/ 180 C and time to 7 minutes.
9. Press MATCH mode, then press start.
10. Serve and enjoy.

Chocolate Brownie Muffins

Cook time: 15 minutes
Serves: 6
Per Serving: Calories 324, Carbs 35g,
Fat 19g, Protein 4.2g

Ingredients:

- Egg - 1
- All-purpose flour - 3/4 cup
- Cocoa powder - 1/4 cup
- Vanilla - 1/2 tsp
- Sugar - 1/2 cup
- Chocolate chips - 1/3 cup
- Baking powder - 1/2 tsp
- Butter, melted - 1/2 cup
- Salt - 1/4 tsp

Directions:

1. In a bowl, whisk egg, sugar, vanilla, and butter.
2. Add remaining ingredients and mix until well combined.
3. Pour batter into the silicone muffin molds.
4. Place a crisper plate in both baskets.
5. Place muffin molds in both baskets, then insert baskets in the unit.
6. Press zone 1, then select air fry mode.
7. Set the temperature to 350 F/ 180 C and time to 15 minutes.
8. Press MATCH mode, then press start.
9. Serve and enjoy.

Easy Semolina Pudding

Cook time: 20 minutes
Serves: 4
Per Serving: Calories 205, Carbs 40g,
Fat 2g, Protein 5g

Ingredients:

- Semolina - 2 oz
- Ground cardamom - 1/2 tsp
- Milk - 2 cups
- Caster sugar - 1/2 cup

Directions:

1. Mix semolina and 1/2 cup milk in a bowl. Slowly add the remaining milk, sugar, and cardamom, and mix well.
2. Pour the mixture into the four greased ramekins.
3. Place a crisper plate in both baskets.
4. Place ramekins in both baskets, then insert baskets in the unit.
5. Press zone 1, then select air fry mode.
6. Set the temperature to 300 F/ 148 C and time to 20 minutes.
7. Press MATCH mode, then press start.
8. Serve and enjoy.

Tasty Apple Fritters

Cook time: 8 minutes
Serves: 10
Per Serving: Calories 170, Carbs 24g,
Fat 6g, Protein 2.7g

Ingredients:

- Bisquick - 2 1/4 cups
- Apples, peel & dice - 2
- Milk - 2/3 cup
- Butter, melted - 2 tbsp
- Cinnamon - 1 tsp
- Sugar - 2 tbsp

Directions:

1. In a bowl, mix Bisquick, sugar, and cinnamon. Add milk and mix until dough forms.
2. Add apple and mix well.
3. Place a crisper plate in both baskets. Line both baskets with parchment paper.
4. Make fritters from the mixture and place them into both baskets.
5. Brush fritters with melted butter, then insert baskets in the unit.
6. Press zone 1, then select air fry mode.
7. Set the temperature to 350 F/ 180 C and the time to 8 minutes.
8. Press MATCH mode, then press start.
9. Serve and enjoy.

CONCLUSION

The Dual-Zone Air Fryer is a super cool kitchen appliance that changes how you cook your favorite food. It allows you to make more than one dish in a single cooking cycle because it has two separate cooking zones.

This cookbook is what helps you become a master in using the dual-zone air fryer. In this cookbook, you will find plenty of great meal recipes that you can cook for your family and friends. Using this cookbook, you will also learn how the air fryer works and how to make delicious dishes.

This cookbook is loaded with 100's of mouthwatering Air fryer recipes.

The recipes in this cookbook come from different categories, like delicious breakfast, lunch, appetizer and side dish, fish and seafood, poultry, meat, vegetables, and desserts.

Enjoy!

This page is for your notes

This page is for your notes

This page is for your notes

This page is for your notes

Printed in Great Britain
by Amazon

36190590R00044